A Search Institute Report

Starting Out Right

Developmental Assets for Children

Nancy Leffert, Ph.D.
Peter L. Benson, Ph.D.
Jolene L. Roehlkepartain

Foreword by Ann S. Masten, Ph.D.
Institute of Child Development, University of Minnesota

Thresher Square West
Suite 210
700 South Third Street
Minneapolis, MN
55415

Starting Out Right is dedicated to our children, Jonathan and Jeremy Leffert, Liv and Kai Munson-Benson, and Micah and Linnea Roehlkepartain, for all they have taught us about development.

Acknowledgments

The authors thank members of the children's assets development committee in St. Louis Park, Minn., for their time and energy in laying some of the initial groundwork for creating children's assets. The authors also thank Louise Bates Ames, Ph.D., Martha Farrell Erickson, Ph.D., Mary Sheedy Kurcinka, Jean Illsley Clarke, Connie Dawson, Ph.D., and Judy Carter for their helpful comments in defining the assets for children at different ages. In addition, the authors are grateful to Daniel J. Repinski, Ph.D., W. Andrew Collins, Ph.D., Brenda Holben, and Ellen Albee for their careful reading of earlier drafts of this manuscript, as well as to our colleagues at Search Institute: Dale A. Blyth, Ph.D., Jennifer Griffin-Wiesner, Eugene C. Roehlkepartain, Peter C. Scales, Ph.D., and Kate Tyler.

This report has been prepared as part of Search Institute's national Healthy Communities • Healthy Youth initiative, which seeks to equip communities to support the positive development of children and adolescents. Support for this initiative is provided by Lutheran Brotherhood, a not-for-profit financial services organization. Lutheran Brotherhood provides financial services and community service opportunities for Lutherans nationwide, as well as philanthropic outreach in communities. For more information on the Healthy Communities • Healthy Youth initiative, call Search Institute at 1-800-888-7828.

Starting Out Right: Developmental Assets for Children

By Nancy Leffert, Ph.D., Peter L. Benson, Ph.D., and Jolene L. Roehlkepartain

Search Institute
700 South Third Street, Suite 210
Minneapolis, MN 55415
http://www.search-institute.org
Telephone: (612) 376-8955
Toll free: 1-800-888-7828
Fax: (612) 376-8956
E-mail: search@search-institute.org

© 1997 by Search Institute

Printed on recycled paper in the United States of America
January 1997

10   9   8   7   6   5   4   3   2

Credits

Editor: Kate Tyler
Graphic Designer: Connie G. Baker

ISBN   1-57482-364-7

Contents

Figures

Foreword   by Ann S. Masten, Ph.D.

s the 20th century draws to a close, there is a growing sense of urgency about the well-being of children in the United States, as well as in many other countries of the world. The "infrastructure" for child development is threatened by massive changes in the structure of the family, community, workplace, society, and international affairs. Danger signs abound in swelling numbers of homeless families and children growing up in unremitting poverty, rising rates of child abuse, increasing violent crime among youth at younger and younger ages, growing risks for death among youth by homicide and suicide, increasing substance abuse among children and adolescents, and the growing phenomenon of childbirth among young women barely out of childhood, with little education, financial support, or social support. It would be easy to despair in response to this gloomy picture, and the greatest danger our children face in these times may be the risk of adults and society giving up—"what could I possibly do that would make any difference?"

This volume offers a voice of hope and a practical guide for every person and community wondering what they can do to restore and strengthen the protective systems for healthy child development. It provides a framework for "asset building" on behalf of children in families and communities. The framework has been developed by Search Institute on the basis of extensive research and consultation with many experts in education, child development, and community action, as well as their experience implementing proactive, asset-focused initiatives in communities throughout the United States.

The asset-enhancing model put forward in this guide is highly congruent with the message emerging from two decades of research on resilience in children at risk. Diverse studies of children who succeed when there is good reason to expect otherwise have implicated key protective factors for child development. At the top of that list are the relationships children have with competent, responsive, caring adults, beginning with parents and extended family, and expanding as the world of the child expands to school and community. The literature on children who make it in spite of poverty, neglect or maltreatment, violent neighborhoods, and all the many other hazards that threaten development—who succeed in school and eventually in their work outside of or inside the home, become prosocial and responsible individuals, care about others, and develop the skills to negotiate life's challenges—indicates that these children generally have more resources.

Overcoming adversity does not occur by magic; studies show that resilience is more likely when a child has more assets within the individual, the home, the school, and the community. Good parents and care (from parents and others) is particularly crucial in the early years when attachment relationships profoundly influence fundamental beliefs a child has about self and others. Caregivers function as assets in many different ways, as suggested by the lists of developmental assets found in this guide, but teachers, neighbors, and other adults in the daily lives of children often play a critical role, particularly when parents, for whatever reason, are unable to protect their children.

Resilient children develop good problem-solving skills and believe in their own abilities to master challenges, which suggests another set of important developmental assets covered in this guide. Adequate nutrition, health care, and early opportunities to learn and succeed, for example, all foster the development of a child's intellectual skills and self-confidence.

As the authors are careful to point out, we still have much to learn about fostering better developmental outcomes in children and youth. Many of the authors' suggestions are based on research with adolescents or speculation about how assets actually influence child development. Little information is available at this time about the specific effectiveness of asset building for young children. A large body of research on children and resilience suggests that this strategy has great potential, however. Above all, this approach has value in opening a practical and hopeful dialogue among individuals, communities, and policy makers about what children need for healthy development and what each person can contribute to the goal of meeting those needs. The actions we take now to rebuild and strengthen the infrastructure for child development are likely to determine the well-being of our society as well as our children in the next century.

Ann S. Masten, Ph.D., is associate professor of education and associate director of the Institute of Child Development at the University of Minnesota, Twin Cities. She has been conducting research on children's issues since the mid-1970s. She has directed three major resiliency projects, including a continuing study that began in 1976 on why some children thrive in unexpected circumstances.

Setting the Stage

Chapters 1 and 2 focus on the framework of the 40 developmental assets and how those assets were developed for children.

Chapter 1   Rebuilding the Foundation for Healthy Child Development

 hildhood in the United States is full of paradoxes. The nation consumes a vast quantity of the world's resources, yet one-fourth of the nation's children live in poverty. Many children have unprecedented access to communication technology, yet few have people they can talk with about things that matter to them. Adults spend billions of dollars each year on toys, games, and designer clothes for children, but spend far too little time building relationships with children, playing with them, and listening to them. Nearly everyone knows the importance of surrounding children with caring, responsible adults, yet many children are left unsupervised, with the mass media as a primary source of guidance.

These kinds of paradoxes rarely make the headlines or galvanize the public into action. But they represent—in the words of the Carnegie Task Force on Meeting the Needs of Young Children—a "quiet crisis"[2] that is eroding the foundation that children need to "start out right" in life. Too few children experience supportive, caring relationships in their families and with people around them. Too few children receive adequate guidance or the positive opportunities that can help them to make positive choices. And too few children receive constant and consistent nurturing of the values, commitments, and competencies they need to become independent, contributing members of society.

Meanwhile, increasing public concern has been directed at problem behaviors among children—including alcohol and other drug use, violence and victimization, and delinquency.[3] There is growing public anxiety about the long-term health of our society if we do not provide children and adolescents with the foundation they need to grow up healthy, caring, and responsible. Marian Wright Edelman of the Children's Defense Fund eloquently captures the depth and breadth of our cultural dilemma:

> *Never have we exposed children so early and relentlessly to cultural messages glamorizing violence, sex, possessions, alcohol and tobacco*

with so few mediating influences from responsible adults. Never have we experienced such a numbing and reckless reliance on violence to solve problems, feel powerful, or be entertained. Never have so many children been permitted to rely on guns and gangs rather than on parents, neighbors, religious congregations, and schools for protection and guidance. Never have we pushed so many children onto the tumultuous sea of life without the life vests of nurturing families and communities, caring schools, challenged minds, job prospects and hope.

As we face a new century and a new millennium, the overarching challenge for America is to rebuild a sense of community and hope and civility and caring and safety for all of our children.[4]

▼ Naming the Building Blocks

If the foundation for children is crumbling, what do we need to do to rebuild it? What are the key building blocks that our children need for a positive start in life? With this report, Search Institute offers an exploratory framework for understanding and building the foundation that children from birth to age 11 need to begin a healthy life. For each major age group of children (infants and toddlers, preschoolers, and elementary school-age children), we describe the "developmental assets" that form this foundation.

(Although we refer in this report to "elementary-age children," we recognize that 10- and 11-year-olds are considered by many scholars as young adolescents and that most 11-year-olds are in middle school, not elementary school, in sixth grade. For the sake of brevity, we use the term *elementary-age children* as shorthand for "elementary-school children and early middle-school youth.")

Search Institute introduced the concept of developmental assets for youth ages 12 to 18 in its 1990 research report *The Troubled Journey: A Portrait of 6th–12th Grade Youth.*[5] This report demonstrated that 30 developmental assets were powerful influences in adolescents' lives, based on a study of 47,000 6th- to 12th-grade students across the United States who were surveyed about their attitudes and behaviors. The assets were organized into two dimensions—internal assets and external assets—and six categories within those dimensions: support, boundaries, structured time use, educational commitment, positive values, and social competencies.

Between 1989 and 1995, Search Institute verified the importance of the asset framework through studies of more than 250,000 6th- to 12th-grade youth in more than 450 communities nationwide. The institute's research has documented that the more assets a young person has, the less likely he or she is to engage in or experience a wide range of negative behaviors, including violence, early sexual intercourse, school problems, and the use of alcohol and other drugs. Furthermore, these assets promote positive outcomes such as doing well in school, having successful peer relationships, and volunteering in the community. The average young person, however, experiences only 16.5 of these 30 assets, according to the institute's research.[6]

In 1996, Search Institute introduced an expanded framework of 40 assets for the 12- to 18-year-old age group; it restructured some of the original assets, renamed a few of the categories, and added two new categories of assets: empowerment and positive identity. (See page 98 for a list of the 40 developmental assets framed for adolescents.) Preliminary data based on this expanded model show that the 40 assets are related to a young person's behaviors and choices in much the same way as are the 30 assets—that is, that the presence of the assets in a young person's life is strongly related to her or his behaviors and choices.[7]

As communities have learned about the assets of the youth in their schools, many have begun community-wide efforts to strengthen the developmental foundation for youth, using the asset framework as a guide. Search Institute has begun a national initiative to support such local efforts. In this context, the need for a congruent framework for younger children became clear. People could see that assets for adolescence built on a foundation established in childhood. Moreover, people also perceived that the asset language offered a helpful lens for understanding child development issues. As a result, a growing number of individuals and organizations asked Search Institute for help in extending the developmental asset model to younger children.

▼ How We Developed the Children's Assets

To develop the developmental asset framework for children from birth to age 11, Search Institute asked new questions based on what our researchers already knew about the importance of assets for adolescents: What are the roots of each of the 40 assets? What do these assets look like in infancy? at age five? at age 11? How do adults nurture these assets over time?

With these questions in mind, we consulted child- and youth-development practitioners, researchers, and the scientific literature in the fields of child development, prevention, resiliency, public health, education, community development, and social change. We also assembled a local committee of educators, school administrators, and early childhood and family education experts that met regularly for six months to help us develop a framework that would communicate clearly to parents and practitioners.[8] We then asked national experts to review and refine the framework.[9]

▼ The Scope of the Assets

The framework presented here blends Search Institute's seven-year effort to name the developmental assets for adolescents[10] with the extensive literature in child development and the practical wisdom of people who have dedicated their lives to understanding and caring for children. We use the framework of developmental assets for adolescents as a lens for identifying what the assets might look like in younger children. Our work represents a well-informed first step in conceptualizing the developmental assets for children from birth to age 11.

The assets are not an exhaustive list of what children may need to grow up healthy. In addition, the asset framework is only one of many ways to organize or conceptualize an understanding of children's needs. Our framework of assets is one model of children's necessary developmental building blocks, one that we believe is applicable across gender, family income, geographic location, and race and ethnicity. The assets may look different for—or some may be particularly important with—certain subgroups of children, such as children with learning disabilities or with behavioral or emotional problems.

The developmental assets do not directly address many factors that interfere with children's healthy development. Poverty, abuse, neglect, and other serious problems that many children experience can impede development. The developmental assets emphasize relationships, social experiences, social environments, patterns of interaction, and norms over which people have considerable control. As a result, the assets are more about the primary processes of socialization, and the contexts in which they occur, than the equally important arenas of economy, housing, services, and the "bricks and mortar" of a city. We know from our own and others' research on adolescents, however, that human developmental and relational factors are critical for adolescents to grow up healthy. The developmental assets address these needs and offer a useful tool to promote positive youth outcomes.[11]

In expanding the adolescent asset framework to children, we have preserved the eight overarching asset categories: support, empowerment, boundaries and expectations, constructive use of time, commitment to learning, positive values, social competencies, and positive identity. We also have maintained consistency in the individual 40 assets across all age groups, establishing a common thread from infancy through age 18. At the same time, the 40 assets have been defined in ways that capture the specific needs of children at each stage of development: infants and toddlers (birth to age 2); preschoolers (ages 3 to 5); and elementary school-age children (ages 6 to 11). These distinctions recognize the major differences in the development of, for example, the preschooler versus a fifth-grader, or the infant versus the first-grader. The complete birth-through-adolescence framework reflects a natural, developmentally appropriate progression across the age groups.

> *"A good start marks the beginning of hope. A poor start can leave an enduring legacy of impairment, and the high costs may show up in the various systems of health care, education, and juvenile justice. We call these impairments by many names: disease, disability, ignorance, incompetence, hatred, violence. By whatever name, such outcomes entail severe economic and social penalties for the nation."[12]*
>
> David A. Hamburg
> President,
> Carnegie Corporation of New York

▼ Cautions in Using the Asset Framework with Children

Search Institute's framework of developmental assets for adolescents has become a powerful focal point for community action and education. Extending this framework to children is our first attempt to construct a consistent, developmentally based road map for understanding and addressing the needs of young people from birth through the teenage years. The children's asset framework offers one set of benchmarks to measure how we as a society care for our children. It also provides useful tools for parents, caregivers, educators, and others to reflect on their role in children's lives.

Our model of children's assets is, however, preliminary. Extensive research and empirical testing would be needed before we would have the same confidence in the children's asset framework that we have in the framework for adolescents. Search Institute has not developed tools to measure these assets in children. Indeed, measuring assets in children poses significant challenges. The adolescent assets are measured using self-report surveys of youth that require a sixth-grade reading comprehension, which are not directly useable with young children.

The framework here is only a beginning conceptualization; it is theoretical and exploratory. Nevertheless, because our children's asset model is based on extensive literature in child development and on the experience of practitioners as well as on our research with adolescents, we believe it provides a useful starting point for extending Search Institute's asset-building model into childhood. We do not intend this report to offer the final word on everything children need to form a healthy foundation. Instead, we expect—and hope—that our model will evolve through inquiry and dialogue among scholars and practitioners, and that it prompts research to refine the developmental building blocks from birth to age 18.[13]

▼ What You Will Find in this Report

Starting Out Right begins with an overview of the framework of developmental assets for children; this chapter also notes some key themes within the asset framework. In chapter two, we provide a more thorough explanation of the eight asset types. The eight chapters that follow each examine an asset category (support, boundaries and expectations, etc.), explaining the assets within each category in light of developmental differences across the various age groups. They are followed by charts of the assets for each age group.

All of the assets, while theoretically based, are empirically derived from our research on adolescents and the research of others in the field. Some of the assets, however, have a more extensive empirical foundation than others. We provide an overview of the research that pertains to specific assets while pointing out areas where more research may be needed. Where similarities exist among assets, we have combined some of our explanations.

FIGURE 1

Factors for Healthy Child Development

What factors contribute to healthy development? The Carnegie Task Force on Meeting the Needs of Young Children lists a number of factors that are consistent with the children's assets we present in this report.

◆ A close and caring nuclear family that sticks together, even during times of stress.

◆ A relationship with at least one parent who unconditionally loves, nurtures, and teaches the child skills, values, and consistent boundaries.

◆ Easy access to nurturing and supportive extended family.

◆ A supportive community, such as a caring neighborhood, a nurturing ethnic group, or a supportive religious, school, or community organization.

◆ Parents who receive explicit and implicit parenting education so they understand and have at their disposal practical tips for raising children through each developmental phase.

◆ A positive outlook on the future, which gives the child hope.

◆ A predictable home environment where the child feels safe to take advantage of opportunities in the environment.

Information from Carnegie Task Force on Meeting the Needs of Young Children, *Starting Points: Meeting the Needs of Our Youngest Children* (Waldorf, Md.: Carnegie Corporation of New York, 1984), vii.

Chapter 2   What Children Need: An Overview of Developmental Assets

ecent years have seen a plethora of information emerge on the healthy development of children, focusing on effective parenting and parent education, quality child care and schools, responsive health care and other themes. Furthermore, this information has been applied in a wide variety of contexts, including highly visible national programs such as Head Start, Success by Six, and other early childhood and family education programs.

These efforts—some of which have been more successful than others—have focused considerable energy on addressing children's needs at critical times in their development. What has been missing, however, is a broad picture of how these pieces fit together —that is, a multifaceted vision of healthy child and adolescent development in which everyone in a community sees his or her role in contributing to the well-being of young people.

The developmental asset framework embodies such a wide vision. In establishing benchmarks for positive child and youth development, the asset model pertains to all aspects of a young person's life, including family, school, and community influences. The asset framework enables individuals and systems to use a common language and employ complementary strategies toward a shared goal—healthy children and youth. The asset model also challenges communities to build new strengths that are needed to ensure that all children and adolescents have access to the opportunities, relationships, and resources they need to form a solid foundation for life. When combined with Search Institute's previous work on developmental assets for 12- to 18-year-olds, the assets identified for children in this report offer a comprehensive vision of what young people need in the first two decades of life to become healthy, caring, responsible, and contributing members of our society.

On pages 24–25 is a chart that depicts the framework of assets and shows the assets' progression from infancy through the teenage years across four age groups: infants/toddlers, preschoolers, elementary school age, and adolescence. The assets are arranged into eight categories that reflect the expanded framework of 40 adolescent assets introduced by Search Institute in 1996.[14] The categories are support, empowerment, boundaries and expectations, constructive use of time, commitment to learning, positive values, social competencies, and positive identity.

In the asset framework, the categories are organized along two dimensions: external assets and internal assets:

FIGURE 2

Developmental Asset Categories

External Assets

♦ Support

♦ Empowerment

♦ Boundaries and expectations

♦ Constructive use of time

Internal Assets

♦ Commitment to learning

♦ Positive values

♦ Social competencies

♦ Positive identity

- **External assets** are factors that surround young people with the support, empowerment, boundaries, expectations, and opportunities that guide them to behave in healthy ways and to make wise choices. These assets are provided by many people and social contexts, including families, schools, neighbors, religious congregations, and organizations. The external-asset categories are support, empowerment, boundaries and expectations, and constructive use of time.

- **Internal assets** are the commitments, values, competencies, and self-perceptions that must be nurtured within young people to provide them with "internal compasses" to guide their behaviors and choices. The four internal-asset categories are commitment to learning, positive values, social competencies, and positive identity.

While the external/internal distinction is useful for clearly understanding the asset categories, the distinction is not directly applicable to infants and young children. During infancy and early childhood, *all* of the assets essentially *externally surround* the child through important relationships. Infants, toddlers, and preschoolers are more dependent on adults than are older children. For this reason, the asset definitions for infants and young children put the responsibility for building both external and internal assets in the hands of parents and other caregivers.

Children typically do not begin to have the cognitive or emotional abilities to internalize behaviors, values, and competencies—the internal assets—until ages six to nine.[15] They develop these values and competencies through a slow process of observation, social learning, and internalization, a process that continues through early and middle adolescence. Early childhood experiences can provide a foundation for children to internalize these assets as they develop cognitive, moral, and social capacities.

▼ External Assets

Positive development requires constant exposure to interlocking systems of support, empowerment, boundaries and expectations, and constructive use of time. The first 20 developmental assets provide this essential web of safety and support.

- **Support**—Support refers to the ways children are loved, affirmed, and accepted. Ideally, children experience an abundance of support not only in their families but also from many other people in a variety of settings. Infants and children will receive this support mainly in their families, but they also should experience this support in child care settings, in preschool, in religious congregations, among extended family, within the family's social network, in neighborhoods, and in other arenas of socialization.

- **Empowerment**—A key developmental need for a child is to feel safe and valued. The empowerment assets focus on community perceptions of children and the opportunities available for children to contribute to society in meaningful ways.

- **Boundaries and expectations**—For healthy development, clear and consistently maintained boundaries need to complement the support and empowerment children receive. Ideally, the boundary assets are experienced in the settings of family, school, child care, and the neighborhood. They provide a set of consistent messages about appropriate behavior across socializing contexts. In addition, children benefit from adults' having appropriately high expectations of them. These expectations challenge children to excel and enhance their sense of competence.

- **Constructive use of time**—One of the prime characteristics of a healthy community for children is a rich array of constructive opportunities for children as young as seven or eight and for families with younger children. Ensuring good after-school supervision for school-age children has become particularly important as more and more parents of both sexes work outside of the home. Whether through schools, community organizations, religious institutions, or for-profit centers, structured activities stimulate positive growth and also contribute to the development of other assets.

▼ Internal Assets

A community's responsibility for its children does not stop with the provision of external assets. Communities must also nurture the internalized commitments, values, competencies, and identity needed to guide choices and create a sense of "centeredness" and purpose. Adults who model these assets when children are young lay the foundation for children to observe, learn, and gradually internalize the assets as they grow.

- **Commitment to learning**—A commitment to learning and education is essential to children, especially in today's fast-changing world. Developing an internal intellectual curiosity and the skills to gain new knowledge is important for success in school and eventually for entering a work force marked by rapid change. The foundations for learning and education are set during infancy through the beliefs and behaviors of the parent and caregiver.

- **Positive values**—Positive values are important "internal compasses" to guide children's priorities and choices. Though there are many values that American society cherishes and seeks to nurture in children, the asset framework focuses on widely shared values that affect children's behaviors.

- **Social competencies**—These assets are some of the important personal and interpersonal skills children need to negotiate through the maze of choices, options, and relationships they face. These skills also lay a foundation for independence and competence as adults.

- **Positive identity**—The final asset category focuses on children's views of themselves—their own sense of agency, purpose, worth, and promise. Without a positive sense of who they are, children risk feeling powerless, without a sense of initiative and direction.

▼ How Do Assets Develop?

> *"Over the last decade or so, 'wars' have been proclaimed, in turn, on teen pregnancy, dropping out, drugs, and most recently violence …. Instead of more such 'wars,' what we need is to follow the logic of prevention, offering our children the skills for facing life that will increase their chances of avoiding any and all of these fates."*[16]
>
> *Daniel Goleman, Ph.D.*
> *Behavioral specialist and author*

Two questions from the field of child development are particularly relevant to the question of how assets develop throughout infancy, early childhood, elementary school, and adolescence: 1) Is development a result of *nature* or *nurture*? 2) Is development a *continuous* process?

The nature-vs.-nurture question focuses on whether children are a product of their genetic makeup (nature) or a product of their upbringing and their life experiences (nurture). Although many in the field lean a little toward one side or the other, most developmentalists agree that development is affected by a lifelong interaction of nature and nurture.[17] Children grow up within a system;[18] within that system, development occurs through continual *transactions* between the child's constitution (such as temperament) and the quality and reciprocal nature of the child's environment. These transactions occur across time.[19]

The question of whether development is continuous or discontinuous focuses on *how*, exactly, children develop. Is development a gradual process in which an infant's skills or abilities are directly related to skills and abilities later in life? Or is development a set of unrelated steps? Most developmentalists agree that development is a continuous process with early experiences and opportunities helping to shape later ones. That does not mean, however, that the way a child behaves in adolescence is necessarily predetermined by early childhood experiences; events may occur that could alter the course of development.[20]

e believe that the process of asset development is continuous and that it involves a complex interaction of nature and nurture. External assets (such as support and empowerment) are essential in the early months and years, and they are helpful in building the internal assets (such as positive values and positive identity formation). Infants take in their world by what they see, hear, and feel. Although an infant does not have the "ability" to be honest or responsible, the infant begins to learn about these values by observing the behaviors of her or his parents and by the caring, honest, and responsible ways in which parents and caregivers care for the infant.

The young child also begins to sense the parents' views about themselves and the world. These feelings and attitudes gradually become internalized by the child as part of his or her world view. When the child develops the capacity to communicate verbally, adults and young children begin to talk about feelings and beliefs, although these conversations are simple and concrete in the early childhood and elementary school years. Children also observe adults talking and acting in consistent ways, which adds to children's slow process of internalization. During the elementary school years, verbal skills and reasoning ability increase, opening the door for more explanatory and in-depth conversations between adults and children.

The child's social relationships are essential to her or his asset development. During infancy, most of the infant's time is spent with her or his immediate family and with one or two additional primary caregivers if the infant goes to a child care setting. When a child goes to preschool and then to elementary school, she or he spends more and more time away from the parent's direct supervision. Asset development is strengthened—and parents' childrearing jobs are easier—when children's experiences in these socializing systems are consistent with the parent(s') asset-building messages.

▼ How Many Assets Do Children Need?

How many of the assets do children need to be healthy? Until research confirms the usefulness of this framework for children, this question is difficult to answer. Certainly, we cannot expect *all* children to experience *all* of the assets all of the time. Nonetheless, our data on adolescents suggests that the more a child experiences or possesses these assets, the better the chance that he or she will grow up to be a healthy, caring, responsible, and contributing member of society.

A reasonable goal might be for children to experience 31 or more of the 40 developmental assets for their age group.[21] This recommendation is consistent with the asset goals suggested by Search Institute's research involving adolescents. The institute's research on adolescents has shown a small, but observable, decrease in assets among older adolescents (9th- through 12th-graders) as compared with young adolescents (6th- through 8th-graders).[22] It is possible that young children need more assets than do adolescents; this would need to be confirmed by research. We might speculate that the lower asset level that we observe when comparing older adolescents with young adolescents is a continuation of a decreasing trend originating in childhood. It could be, for example, that many infants begin their lives surrounded by many assets in their environment and that asset availability in their lives subsequently begins a slow downward progression. This could happen inevitably, as children bump up against a myriad of positive and negative experiences; also, children could be particularly vulnerable to negative experiences because of their immaturity. If this speculation were confirmed empirically, it would only underscore the importance of intentional asset building in the lives of the youngest members of our society.

▼ What Does the Children's Asset Framework Offer?

Much of the information about asset building will seem familiar—or even intuitive—to parents, teachers, and others concerned with child development. The asset framework distills the best available knowledge, from many different sources, about what young people need. As such, the framework offers several benefits:

1. It **affirms** what many people already do well. In a society that focuses almost exclusively on problems and problem-solving, the asset model highlights the positive things that many people can provide to children, and that all children need to grow up to be competent, caring, and responsible.

2. It **communicates** clearly to many different audiences, making it a useful tool for educating parents and others about the needs of children. The asset model can be a helpful reminder of childrearing priorities and values that may have been common wisdom in the past, but which may have been neglected or forgotten in today's more complex world.

3. It suggests a **common ground** around which many people and institutions can unite for the benefit of children and the community. Communities that have begun asset-building initiatives for adolescents have found that the assets offer a shared language for people from many different backgrounds and perspectives. Extending the asset framework to children has the potential to expand and strengthen community education and action for all young people.

4. It offers a **new barometer** for assessing the well-being of children. Many, if not all, of the current measures of well-being in childhood focus on whether children have specific problems. One example is the *Kids Count* report released annually by the Annie E. Casey Foundation. This highly influential barometer of well-being among children and youth focuses exclusively on monitoring state-by-state trends in 10 areas: low birth-weight babies, infant deaths, child deaths, teen violent deaths, teens having babies, youth arrested for violent crimes, school dropouts, unemployed teens, child poverty, and single-parent

FIGURE 3

Nurturing Children from the Beginning

What do children need to succeed from the very beginning? The Children, Youth, and Family Consortium at the University of Minnesota has identified a number of "protective factors"— which are similar to Search Institute's "assets"—arranged in order of a child's development – from infancy through adolescence. These include:

◆ Prenatal care

◆ Secure attachment between parent and infant

◆ Ongoing involvement of caring adults

◆ Strong connections to school

◆ Competence in at least one area

◆ Service

◆ Personal faith or an affiliation with a religious community

Researchers have found that the early factors have exponential effects: "Secure attachment results in an eagerness to explore and willingness to cooperate, which in turn leads to engagement in school and positive relations with peers and teachers."

Information from Children, Youth, and Family Consortium, "Tipping The Balance Toward Promise," *Seeds of Promise* 1, no. 1 (St. Paul: University of Minnesota, April 1996), 3.

families.[23] Although it is important for us as a society to be aware of the problems and risks confronting young people, it is equally important for us to have a sense of how we are doing in equipping our children with the assets they need to avoid problems and lead productive, meaningful lives.

5. Finally, the asset framework offers **hope**. Today's prevailing emphasis on problems can cause people to feel despair and hopelessness; many problems are large and may seem intractable. By focusing on positive youth development and by demonstrating the power of individuals to make a difference in young people's lives, Search Institute's asset-building framework offers individuals and communities a highly constructive—and hopeful—approach to developing healthy youth and healthy communities. The asset model takes a proactive approach to problems, risks, and needs in the lives of youth; it focuses on what children need to navigate *successfully* through childhood and adolescence.

This emphasis does not minimize the need to address deeply entrenched problems such as poverty, abuse, neglect, homelessness, delinquency, and poor school performance. Research has shown, however, that caring and supportive relationships, core competencies, and other resources can serve as powerful protective factors in the face of other challenges. For example, when Emmy Werner and her colleagues studied a cohort of children from birth until adulthood on the island of Kauai, Hawaii,[24] they found that young people who did well had the support of neighborhood mentors, who were often unrelated to the young people they mentored. Researcher Michael Rutter and his colleagues in Great Britain have found that young people in dysfunctional settings were at lower risk of psychiatric disorder if each had one good relationship.[25]

Ann S. Masten, Karen M. Best, and Norman Garmezy also have studied the resilience of children and adolescents growing up in adverse conditions. They, too, report that children who experience exposure to chronic adversity have better outcomes if they have positive relationships with competent adults, are good learners and problem-solvers, are engaging to or liked by other people, and have a feeling of competence or self-efficacy.[26] Thus, even under adverse living conditions, relationships between children and adults that are supportive, continuous, and of substantial intensity can provide children and youth with the attention and guidance that they need to grow up healthy.

▼ What Are the Implications of Developmental Assets for Children?

Taken as a whole, the developmental asset framework represents a new paradigm for caring for children in our society. It involves a shift away from a focus on the negative to an emphasis on the positive. The asset model suggests that everyone and all sectors of society can—and should—play an active role in contributing to the healthy development of our children and youth.

Several themes have emerged in Search Institute's work on adolescent asset building. We believe these themes are equally relevant to the children's assets and have implications for how communities, organizations, and individuals use the assets:

- **All children need assets.** Every child in the United States needs to experience these assets. All children need both external assets—which are the contextual elements of our families, schools, and communities that foster the child's adaptation to an ever-changing world—and internal assets—the supports and competencies available to each child that foster adaptation. Thus, instead of focusing energy only on specific groups of children (such as those labeled "at risk"), efforts should be made to ensure that *all* children have the necessary developmental assets.

- **Assets are built primarily through relationships.** The most important experiences for children occur in caring relationships. There is no substitute for these relationships. Efforts to build assets should thus focus on providing children with caring relationships everywhere they go. This can occur in families, schools, child care settings, religious congregations, and neighborhoods.

- **Everyone has a role to play.** Because assets are nurtured primarily through relationships, everyone in a community can play a role in asset building. The assets highlight the need for caring families, caring neighbors, and caring institutions. Although professionals certainly have a role, it is just as important that neighbors, friends, relatives, and others see themselves as guardians of our young. (Even in early childhood, when it is important that a limited number of people provide consistent care, others in the community play a role in helping parents and other primary caregivers make it a top priority to nurture their relationships with children.)

- **Building assets is an ongoing process.** Asset building begins before birth, by equipping parents-to-be with skills and knowledge to care for the newborn, and continues throughout adolescence and into adulthood. Although child development experts agree that the first three years of life are essential in giving the child a strong developmental foundation, these early years are not alone sufficient to provide the child with an adequate foundation for life. That foundation must be reinforced, reshaped, and expanded through each phase of development. Furthermore, as discussed earlier, events can occur in a child's life that can alter the course of development.[27] A child who lives in an environment of extreme developmental disadvantage could have his or her life course altered by a caring and committed relationship with an adult. Or a child could have a strong early foundation and then suffer a disabling accident or the death of a parent, "acts of fate" that could change the child's developmental path.

- **Asset building requires consistent messages.** For assets to become a part of children's lives, children need to hear and experience consistent messages from many places. A teacher's affirmation of a child's worth will be undermined if the child hears a different message from a parent or another significant adult. Similarly, parents are undermined in their struggle to teach a young child to resolve conflict peacefully when the media barrage the home with images of violence.

- **Duplication and repetition are valued.** Although there are legitimate reasons to be concerned about unnecessary duplication of services for children and families, it would be impossible to provide too many asset-building experiences for children. Children need to receive dozens of expressions of care, guidance, and opportunities every day in all areas of their lives. Rather than designating one part of asset building to a particular segment of the community (for example, families or schools), everyone in the community must recognize their individual responsibilities for strengthening the child's asset foundation.[28]

FIGURE 4
The Progression of Developmental Assets from Infancy to Adolescence (Birth to age 18)

Asset Type	Infants and Toddlers (Birth to age 2)	Preschoolers (Ages 3 to 5)	Elementary-Age Children (Ages 6 to 11)	Adolescents (Ages 12 to 18)
E X T E R N A L A S S E T S				
Support				
1.	Family support			
2.	Positive family communication			
3.	Other adult resources		Other adult relationships	
4.	Caring neighborhood			
5.	Caring out-of-home climate		Caring school climate	
6.	Parent involvement in out-of-home situations		Parent involvement in schooling	
Empowerment				
7.	Children valued		Community values children	Community values youth
8.	Children have roles in family life	Children given useful roles		Youth as resources
9.	Service to others			
10.	Safety			
Boundaries and Expectations				
11.	Family boundaries			
12.	Out-of-home boundaries		School boundaries	
13.	Neighborhood boundaries			
14.	Adult role models			
15.	Positive peer observation	Positive peer interactions		Positive peer influence
16.	Expectations for growth		High expectations	
Constructive Use of Time				
17.	Creative activities			
18.	Out-of-home activities		Child programs	Youth programs
19.	Religious community			
20.	Positive, supervised time at home		Time at home	

Continued

The Progression of Developmental Assets from Infancy to Adolescence, Continued

Asset Type	Infants and Toddlers (Birth to age 2)	Preschoolers (Ages 3 to 5)	Elementary-Age Children (Ages 6 to 11)	Adolescents (Ages 12 to 18)
I N T E R N A L A S S E T S				
Commitment to Learning				
21.	Achievement expectation		Achievement motivation	
22.	Engagement expectation		School engagement	
23.	Stimulating activity		Homework	
24.	Enjoyment of learning		Bonding to school	
25.	Reading for pleasure			
Positive Values				
26.	Family values caring		Caring	
27.	Family values equality and social justice		Equality and social justice	
28.	Family values integrity		Integrity	
29.	Family values honesty		Honesty	
30.	Family values responsibility		Responsibility	
31.	Family values healthy lifestyle and sexual attitudes		Healthy lifestyle and sexual attitudes	Restraint
Social Competencies				
32.	Planning and decision-making observation	Planning and decision-making practice	Planning and decision-making	
33.	Interpersonal observation	Interpersonal interactions	Interpersonal competence	
34.	Cultural observation	Cultural interactions	Cultural competence	
35.	Resistance observation	Resistance practice	Resistance skills	
36.	Peaceful conflict resolution observation	Peaceful conflict resolution practice	Peaceful conflict resolution	
Positive Identity				
37.	Family has personal power		Personal power	
38.	Family models high self-esteem		Self-esteem	
39.	Family has a sense of purpose		Sense of purpose	
40.	Family has a positive view of the future		Positive view of personal future	

The External Assets

Chapters 3 through 6 focus on four categories of external assets: support, empowerment, boundaries and expectations, and the constructive use of time. Together, they include 20 individual assets that give children the relationships, environments, and opportunities they need to thrive.

Chapter 3	Being There for Children: The Support Assets

Chapter 3

Being There for Children: The Support Assets

upport refers to the many ways adults love, encourage, comfort, and affirm children. From birth, infants need parents and other caregivers who take the time to be with them, to meet their needs, and to be emotionally available to them. Through mutually gratifying interactions that occur between the child and her or his parents and caregivers, relationships develop; these relationships are essential to a child's positive development. In infancy, the groundwork for attachment is laid as caregivers and infants consistently connect with each other.[29] As children grow, support provides children with the security they need to try new tasks, master new skills, and gain new confidence. Children without support are more apt to feel afraid, insecure, and isolated.

Social changes have made efforts to give children multiple sources of support particularly critical today. Many parents no longer have the time to give the emotional and social supports their children need because they are busy trying to provide the basic physical requirements of food, shelter, medical care, and clothing.[30] This is particularly true in single-parent homes, in which more and more children are growing up. Furthermore, many of the sources of support beyond the nuclear family—extended family, neighbors—are less common in today's mobile, adult-oriented society.

Our framework includes six developmental assets that highlight the importance of support within and beyond the family.

▼ Asset No. 1: Family support

Consistent love, comfort, encouragement, and support are essential for healthy development. Each family may demonstrate its caring in a unique way, but researchers have shown that care must be consistent, positive, and responsive. "Unlike adults who are generally capable of maintaining positive emotional ties with a number of different individuals, unrelated or even hostile to each other,

FIGURE 5

The Power of Caring Adults

Researchers agree that at least one caring adult can make a difference in a child's life.

"The most important finding from our research on kids from a wide variety of backgrounds is that they need a strong sense of caring from at least one competent adult," says Michael Resnick of the University of Minnesota School of Public Health and School of Medicine.

"Children who experience chronic adversity fare better or recover more successfully when they have a positive relationship with a competent adult," says Ann S. Masten of the Institute of Child Development, University of Minnesota.

♦

"The bottom line is that children need to know that they can count on their parents to respond in a sensitive, predictable way to their needs," says Byron Egeland of the Institute of Child Development, University of Minnesota, who has been following 267 high-risk infants in a longitudinal study that began in 1975.

Information from Children, Youth, and Family Consortium, "Researchers Agree on What Kids Need to Succeed," *Seeds of Promise* 1, no.1 (St. Paul: University of Minnesota, April 1996), 2, 5.

children lack the capacity to do so. They will freely love more than one adult only if the individuals in question feel positively to one another," wrote Anna Freud and her colleagues in *Beyond the Best Interests of the Child*.[31]

The importance of consistent care for infants has been studied by researchers for many years. For example, Anna Freud studied children who were evacuated for varied reasons from London to the relative safety of the English countryside during World War II. These children lived in nurseries until the end of the war.[32] Freud observed that the separation from their families was traumatic for infants and children alike. Similarly, psychiatrist René Spitz studied wartime nurseries that had one nurse assigned to every eight babies (a high infant/staff ratio brought about by wartime inadequacies). These babies did not receive adequate and consistent attention, and their environment was sterile and devoid of any kind of stimulation. After three months of separation from their mothers, the infants appeared to have a type of depression, characterized by listlessness, unwillingness to socialize, decreased smiling, and eating disturbances.[33] Anna Freud eloquently wrote, "In the case of evacuation, the danger is represented by the sudden disappearance of all the people whom he knows and loves."[34] Experts generally have agreed that these infants were suffering from the lack of a maternal bond or, more specifically, the disruption of the infant/mother relationship.[35]

A key to family support for children is responding appropriately to the child's needs. Silvia Bell and Mary D. S. Ainsworth revealed that infants of parents who answered the infants' cries immediately and consistently during the first few months of life cried less frequently and for shorter amounts of time than did infants whose parents did not respond quickly.[36] While it is important for parents to be responsive, it also is important for them to introduce predictable routines. Routines involving wake-up times, mealtimes, nap times, and bedtimes are soothing and help babies learn to make transitions from one type of activity to another. It often takes weeks—even months—for infants to adjust to routines. Parents and caregivers can introduce routines early in the infant's life so that they are in place by the time the infant is three to six months old.

As children enter the toddler years, parents need respond less immediately as toddlers and young children learn to delay gratification and to comfort themselves. But parents need to help children find creative ways to deal with their own needs. Even babies can comfort themselves with a soft toy or favorite blanket. In fact, intense attachment to a soft toy, blanket, or bit of cloth represents an important phase of early personality development.[37]

Family support also means that parents and caregivers are sensitive to the changing needs of the child as he or she grows from infancy through the elementary school years. Parents and caregivers can help manage the child's environment to accommodate those needs. For example, even sociable babies usually become wary of strangers at around eight months of age. At this time, the baby may also be particularly sensitive to separations from the caregiver. This is an important developmental milestone called "stranger anxiety;" it means that the baby can tell the difference between his or her primary caregiver and someone else.[38] Sometimes parents are needlessly "embarrassed" by the baby's "behavior," and, as a result, may be insensitive to the baby's need to approach new people gradually.

ll children need safe, stable, and predictable environments. For children in child care and preschool settings, high quality is essential in creating predictability for the child. (High-quality indicators include low turnover of staff, a reasonable child-to-caregiver ratio, caregivers who are warm and responsive, and age-appropriate games and activities.)[39] Children old enough to attend school need teachers who care about them and encourage them to learn and grow.

Family support does not only mean love and encouragement, but it also refers to the ways adults interact with children. Diana Baumrind has done extensive research on parenting style and its effects on the outcomes of children and adolescents.[40] Baumrind found that parents could generally be classified as authoritarian, permissive, or authoritative in terms of parenting style.

Authoritarian parents have many rules, which they strictly enforce, often using punitive or forceful tactics. In contrast, permissive parents, who have a warm style, make few demands on children and do not closely monitor them. Authoritative parents have a more flexible style than do authoritarian or permissive parents. In authoritative homes, children are given reasons for rules, which the parents consistently enforce. Authoritative parents consider children's views and respond to children's changing needs.

Many researchers have examined these three parenting styles and have concluded that children from authoritative homes have clear advantages. These children have high achievement motivation and better social skills when compared with the children of authoritarian parents. Children of authoritative parents also are more self-reliant as adolescents and have greater academic success.[41]

▼ Asset No. 2: Positive family communication

Physical touch is the positive family communication that infants need most. Touch, in the form of infant massage, has been shown to benefit premature infants. In an analysis of 19 separate studies, researcher Tiffany Field found that almost three-quarters of preterm infants were positively affected by massage. They gained more weight and showed better performance on developmental tasks.[42] In another study of infant massage, not only did massaged infants gain more weight than did infants who were not massaged, but they also were more alert and active.[43] Physical touch is important for children of all ages, but displays of physical affection are often confounded by separation issues during the elementary school age years and early adolescence; children may "withdraw" from physical affection or be embarrassed by physical touch or hugs. Unfortunately, many adults conclude that the child no longer wants to communicate with them when the child instead is expressing the need for a different form of communication, such as parental encouragement, guidance, or a listening ear.

One way infants communicate with caregivers is through cues such as crying, fussing, or head-turning. Parents and caregivers should respect the infant's cues and respond immediately. If an infant is hungry, the parents and caregivers should feed the infant; when an infant no longer wants to eat, the parents and caregivers should be responsive, respecting the infant's signal to stop.

As babies and toddlers grow, appropriate communication changes. The development of language enables children to use verbal skills to tell their parents, caregivers, and teachers about their needs. Children at this age begin to be able to seek out their parents for assistance when faced with difficult tasks or situations.

It is also important for parents and other adults to initiate conversations with children. Language development researcher Erika Hoff-Ginsburg found that parents who ask questions of their young children, invite verbal response, and encourage dialogue have children who are quicker to acquire the syntactical rules of language. In addition, these children also recognize more letters and numbers, develop larger vocabularies, and score higher on reading skills in the second grade in comparison with children whose parents do not encourage such conversation. [45]

Another important component of positive family communication is the child's willingness to talk with her or his parents about problems or things she or he needs help with. Children should feel safe seeking out their parents and caregivers for assistance, advice, and counsel. For the toddler, this means asking or gesturing for help with difficult or novel situations and getting an appropriate response from her or his caregiver. [46] By the elementary school years, children can discuss problems with their parent(s) and begin to sort out options for decision-making with assistance, and they should feel respected for their age appropriate abilities in this area. "Compared to younger children, 6- to 12-year-olds thus can solve more difficult, abstract intellectual problems in school and can master increased, more complex responsibilities at home and in other common settings," write W. Andrew Collins, Michael L. Harris, and Amy Susman of the University of Minnesota's Institute of Child Development. [47]

Honesty and humor also are important in positive parent-child communication. Children of all ages need to be told the truth in words they can understand, and they also need to know what to expect when they interact with others. And humor should be in abundance. "Humor is directly related to a child's mastery of the world," says Kenneth L. Kaplan, a child psychiatrist and professor at George Washington University. "From infancy on, humor gives children a way to lessen their fears or deflate their discomfort." [48]

▼ Asset No. 3: Other adult resources and relationships
▼ Asset No. 4: Caring neighborhoods
▼ Asset No. 5: Caring out-of-home climate

These three support assets highlight the importance of support beyond the nuclear family. During infancy, the baby's primary adult resource is the parent or primary caregiver. But the adults and parents caring for the baby need other adult resources, especially when they also have one or more young children in the house. These extra supports are essential, especially when family members are feeling rushed and stressed. Indirectly these resources provide support and care to the baby by providing comfort to the parent. Children and parents

		FIGURE 6	
		Support Assets through the Years	
	Infants and Toddlers (Birth to age 2)	**Preschoolers** (Ages 3 to 5)	**Elementary-Age Children** (Ages 6 to 11)
1.	**Family support**		
	Family life provides high levels of love and support.		
2.	**Positive family communication**		
	Parent(s) communicate with the child in positive ways. Parent(s) respond immediately to the child and respect the child.	Parent(s) and child communicate positively. Child seeks out parent(s) for assistance with difficult tasks or situations.	Parent(s) and child communicate positively. Child is willing to seek advice and counsel from parent(s).
3.	**Other adult resources**		**Other adult relationships**
	Parent(s) receive support from three or more nonparent adults and ask for help when needed. The child receives love and comfort from at least one nonparent adult.	Child receives support from at least one nonparent adult. Parent(s) have support from individuals outside the home.	Child receives support from nonparent adults.
4.	**Caring neighborhood**		
	Child experiences caring neighbors.		
5.	**Caring out-of-home climate**		**Caring school climate**
	Child is in caring, encouraging environments outside the home.		School provides a caring, encouraging environment.
6.	**Parent involvement in out-of-home situations**		**Parent involvement in schooling**
	Parent(s) are actively involved in helping the child succeed in situations outside the home.		Parent(s) are actively involved in helping child succeed in school.

cannot have too many supportive people around them, particularly since social and economic trends have threatened the welfare of parents and consequently the well-being of their children.[49]

In a study of 184 new families with first-born infants, researcher Margaret K. McKim of the University of Guelph in Ontario found that almost all of the families she surveyed sought help from other adults, such as medical doctors, friends, and relatives.[50] McKim concluded, however, that cultural taboos may keep many families from getting the support they need. "There is a pervasive cultural taboo against admitting to concerns or problems when you are the parent of an infant," she writes. "If it is not a medical problem, many assume parental inadequacy. This taboo keeps families away from neighbors, friends and relatives as well as available support services."[51]

Even for infants or toddlers, other adults (for example, grandparents and neighbors) may play a significant role in socialization experiences. Generally, it is during early childhood that children begin spending a greater proportion of their time with adults other than the primary caregiver. That is why it is important for children to have supportive adults other than their parents in their lives, including caring neighbors; the more caring adults a child has, the better.

Much of the research regarding the role of nonparental relationships has focused on children in middle school and adolescents in high school. Researchers have found that as young people grow, the number of nonparental adults in their lives decreases.[52] This does not mean, however, that the importance of these relationships declines as children and adolescents get older.[53] Researchers also have suggested that cultural differences affect these relationships. Which nonparental adults young people seek out may vary by ethnicity[54]. African American young people, for example, seem to seek out extended family for this purpose rather than unrelated adults.[55]

▼ Asset No. 6:   Parent involvement in out-of-home situations

Parental involvement in schooling is a much-touted strategy to enhance children's motivation and achievement.[56] In addition, parental involvement in child care is thought to be one factor contributing to the development of empathy later in life.[57]

Parental involvement in a child's life both at home and in out-of-home situations—such as child care, preschool, school, and after-school activities—is a critical factor in a child's school success at all grade levels.[58] One study found that parents of young children tended to be more involved in their children's school activities than were parents of older children.[59] The researchers speculated that this could reflect parents' feelings that the early years of schooling are particularly important. Also, parents may feel that they are more competent to help younger children than older ones and that it may be appropriate to disengage from involvement in schooling after their children are well established in the educational environment. Nevertheless, it is important that parents stay involved in their children's education even through adolescence.

	FIGURE 7
	Ways to Build Support in Children
Age	**Practical age-appropriate ideas**
0–1	• Encourage parents to hold children and to interact with them during feedings.
	• Respond to children's needs.
	• Delight in each child's growth and development.
1–2	• Cheer children on as they master new skills and be available to comfort and guide them when they become frustrated.
	• Delight in children's discoveries about themselves, other people, and the world.
	• Say "yes" to children more than saying "no."
3–5	• Encourage children's thinking abilities by exposing them to new situations.
	• Play with children, letting them choose the type of play.
	• Find other caring adults to participate regularly in each child's life.
6–11	• Encourage children as they learn new skills.
	• When children and adults disagree, encourage adults to point out that they still care about the children.
	• Answer children's questions.

Chapter 4 Valued and Valuable: The Empowerment Assets

T he second type of external assets involve empowerment. Children who are empowered feel good about themselves and their skills. They grow up in homes where they are treated as individuals with unique strengths and needs and where they are encouraged to act independently in age-appropriate situations. Empowered children feel their actions can make a difference.

Our society, however, tends either to ignore children because they get in the way or, conversely, expects them to act like miniature adults. Children may be saddled with adult responsibilities: When a parent cannot afford child care, nine-year-olds may be expected to feed, bathe, and care for younger siblings while the parent works. At the other extreme, children may not be given meaningful, developmentally appropriate roles. Too often adults assume that children want to focus only on themselves, thus neglecting children's sense of concern about and ability to contribute to their families and communities. In addition, adults do so many things *for* children that children often are left with few opportunities to be useful.

We have identified four empowerment assets, including safety, a necessary precondition for empowerment.

▼ **Asset No. 7: Children valued**
▼ **Asset No. 8: Children given useful roles**

Parents and caregivers need to value and appreciate children. The infant and child should have a central role in family life. Ideally, children should live in communities that also value and celebrate children.

Children who are given useful roles feel they have some control over their environment and that they have something worth contributing. Parents can help children develop independence, self-reliance, and positive self-esteem by involving children in developmentally appropriate household tasks and in age-appropriate family decisions.[60] Children as young as 18 months can help by taking on simple jobs around the home, such as folding napkins in half for a meal or putting away blocks when playtime ends. Children also can have input in simple family decisions, such as helping the family choose places to visit or places to eat on family outings.

Involving even young children in such activities can have a positive effect on parents, too. One study described how preschool teachers demonstrated a household task to children, practiced it with them, and then asked parents to practice with their children. The researchers indicated that parents' perceptions of their child's capabilities were affected by this new routine.[62] Parents became aware that their young children were capable of doing more than they had expected.

Parents and teachers can encourage learning and development through involving children in age-appropriate tasks. They can select a task for the child to do where success is likely, be alert to the child's developmental readiness, include the child in the planning of the task, make sure the child can complete the task easily, divide the task into "child-size" portions, and encourage and reinforce the child's efforts.[63] Through this process, a child can feel valued and empowered.

As children grow, their increasing skills and abilities mean that they can take on more difficult household tasks; by adolescence, they often can participate fully in the chores of family life (such as cooking a meal, mowing the lawn, or doing the laundry).

Although researchers have focused on the importance of valuing children and giving them meaningful roles within the family, many of the same principles extend to community settings such as child-serving organizations and schools. Highlighting ways that children are valued and giving them useful roles in non-family settings is an important part of the empowerment process.

▼ Asset No. 9: Service to others

Service to others is an empowerment asset because children (like adults) find that giving to other people carries rewards. "The benefits of including children as providers of service extend beyond today," write Susan J. Ellis, Anne Weisbord, and Katherine H. Noyes. "In a very real sense, when we involve them as volunteers, we are preparing our youth to become active, responsible, caring citizens."[64]

When families participate in community service together, children observe, learn, and experience the values of caring, equality and social justice, integrity, and responsibility. Volunteering as a family also gives family members a meaningful way to spend time together. "Shared volunteer experiences can lead to better communication and more understanding, supportive relationships," states the Family Matters program of The Points of Light Foundation. "Family volunteering provides a great opportunity for parents to be positive role models and to teach their children the importance and the joy of helping others."[65]

arents begin instilling the asset of service in infants, by focusing on the baby and meeting his or her needs. Children rarely develop the asset of service unless they have experienced the care, love, and support of others and unless they are taught that the world revolves around all people, not just them.[66] As children become toddlers, with increased independence, parents and adults can model this asset by serving and helping others outside of the family. Gradually the family can include the child in these interactions. Finding volunteer opportunities that are meaningful for both adults *and* children can be difficult, however. Activities such as reroofing the house of a low-income family may empower an adult, but will overwhelm a four-year-old. Activities should be geared to the developmental readiness of the child.

Energize, Inc., an international organization founded to help people become involved in community service, describes volunteer projects that children younger than 14 have completed. For example, preschool children, accompanied by adults, went from door to door collecting food for a food shelf. Five-year-olds, teamed with

FIGURE 8		
Empowerment Assets through the Years		
Infants and Toddlers (Birth to age 2)	**Preschoolers** (Ages 3 to 5)	**Elementary-Age Children** (Ages 6 to 11)
7.	**Children valued**	**Community values children**
The family places the child at the center of family life.	Parent(s) and other adults value and appreciate children.	Child feels that the community values and appreciates children.
8.	**Children have roles in family life**	**Children given useful roles**
The family involves the child in family life.	Parent(s) and other adults take child into account when making decisions and gradually include the child in decisions.	Child is included in family decisions and is given useful roles at home and in the community.
9.	**Service to others**	
Parent(s) serve others in the community.	The family serves others in the community together.	Child and parent(s) serve others and the community.
10.	**Safety**	
Child has a safe environment at home, in out-of-home settings, and in the neighborhood.		Child is safe at home, at school, and in the neighborhood.

their parents, welcomed newcomers to an orientation program by handing out printed information and helping with name tags. Preschoolers and their parents took nursing home residents on walks.[67]

Older children can participate in more complex acts of service. A group of third- and fourth-graders can make greeting cards for a Meals on Wheels program. Kindergartners can visit, play with, and feed animals at an animal shelter. Fourth- and fifth-graders can plan a craft day at a senior citizen housing complex. First- and second-graders can work with adults in growing vegetables in a community gardening project.

"When volunteering becomes a natural part of a child's life at an early age, it adds an important dimension to the process of growing up and, ultimately shapes the adult that child becomes," write Ellis, Weisbord, and Noyes of Energize, Inc. "Neither schoolwork nor salaried jobs teach *citizenship* in the hands-on way that volunteering does."[66]

▼ Asset No. 10: Safety

FIGURE 9

Safety and Quality of Child Care

The American Association of Pediatrics recommends that all child care staff be trained in first aid, yet this is required in only 11 states. Only 19 states mandate that child care centers have the child-to-staff ratios at the levels recommended by the National Association for the Education of Young Children (NAEYC): six two-year-olds per staff person.

Information from Children's Defense Fund, *The State of America's Children Yearbook 1995* (Washington, D.C., 1995), 40.

Some children play outdoors in unsafe neighborhoods because they have no other choices. They live in neighborhoods where they can trust no one. Growing up in unsafe or violent environments may also affect the choices children make. For example, research shows that young people who grow up in violent communities or violent families are more likely to become involved in substance abuse.[69]

Compounding the safety issue, children sometimes witness horrific events beyond their developmental understanding. Neil Postman of New York University says that by being exposed too early to "adult problems" such as violence, illness, and death, children are robbed of their childhood.[70]

Being robbed of childhood not only implicates physical safety, but also emotional safety. David Elkind, a professor at Tufts University and the author of many child-rearing books, has coined the term "the hurried child." He contends that many of our children are growing up too fast, which results in their not feeling emotionally safe.[71]

Children grow up feeling safe and secure if they feel able to learn more about themselves, other people, and the world. Young children who are allowed slowly to process the ordinary fears that occur during growing up are more apt to feel good about themselves. Those who are pushed and whose fears are dismissed often feel ashamed and begin to think the world is a scary place.[72]

As children enter school, they slowly begin to spend less time with their parents and to form attachments to their peers. Unfortunately, parents sometimes rush this stage, which can result in fearful children who are ill-equipped to deal with complex life experiences they may face. Children's formation of close friendships is important at this stage, but so is their closeness with parents.

Raising children who feel safe and secure is closely tied to a number of other assets. Children who feel safe are those who have a lot of support. They feel empowered and valued. They feel secure enough to venture forth in the world, to take risks to learn new skills and meet new challenges. And they feel good about themselves.

FIGURE 10
Ways to Empower Children

Age	Practical age-appropriate ideas
0–1	• Encourage parents to prop up babies and hold young children so they can see more.
	• Respond immediately to children's cries and needs.
	• Always monitor children to keep them safe.
1–2	• Encourage the concept of community service by having children do simple tasks that help out at home.
	• Child proof all environments where children play to ensure safety.
	• Show children positive alternatives to inappropriate behaviors.
3–5	• Do simple acts of community service, such as collecting cans of food for a food bank.
	• Give children simple chores, such as sorting laundry by color or matching socks.
	• Teach children basic safety rules, such as avoiding poisons and looking both ways before crossing the street while holding an adult's hand.
6–11	• Ask children how they would like to help others; figure out simple ways for them to carry through on their wishes.
	• Closely monitor children and their activities even though they appear not to need constant, direct supervision.
	• Ask children's opinions about what they like and do not like in their daily routines. Make changes based on some of their ideas.

Chapter 5   Knowing the Limits: The Boundaries-and-Expectations Assets

hildren need to know how to act and how not to act, and they need to hear clear instructions—not conflicting messages—from parents and other caregivers. Boundaries and expectations are part of what makes our society civilized and safe. Homes, schools, organizations, and communities that make an effort to set clear, consistent boundaries encourage the healthy development of children.

In the first half of this century, most American babies were raised on a schedule; they had to wait to be fed until the next scheduled feeding time. Today we know that it is important to respond immediately to infants' cries and to set boundaries and expectations sensitive to children's changing needs. Many babies have established a regular daily rhythm by the time they are three months old. Sleeping through the night often is one of the first boundaries parents or caregivers can set for the child, once the child is physically capable of it.

Children between the ages of 2 and 11 learn many boundaries and expectations, such as toilet training, looking both ways before crossing the street, and returning borrowed items. Through the thousands of interactions between the child and the adults around the child, the child learns what is acceptable and what is not in terms of safety, socialization, and values.

The framework of assets identifies six boundaries and expectations. These address boundaries in different settings, the importance of modeling positive behaviors, and the importance of clear expectations.

▼ Asset No. 11: Family boundaries
▼ Asset No. 12: Out-of-home boundaries
▼ Asset No. 13: Neighborhood boundaries

FIGURE 11

Helpful Ways to Enforce Boundaries

Researchers have found that a number of factors increase toddlers' compliance with boundaries:

◆ The boundary must be understandable to the child.

◆ Adults should be sensitive to the child's feelings when interrupting the child because of a boundary infraction.

◆ Adults should express appreciation to the child when he or she changes behavior.

Information from Sandra R. Kaler and Claire Kopp, "Compliance and Comprehension in Very Young Toddlers," *Child Development* 61 (1990): 1997–2103, and Harriet Rheingold, Kaye Cook, and Vicki Koloqitz, "Commands Activate the Behavior and Pleasure of Two-Year-Old Children," *Developmental Psychology* 23 (1987): 146–51.

Children need to know what constitutes acceptable behavior and what to expect when they venture outside the family standards. Parents and caregivers need not only to set clear boundaries, but also to consistently reinforce them. When children are in child care, preschool, school, or other settings outside the home, they need to know the boundaries and expectations pertinent to each situation. Ideally, these standards would be consistent with ones the child receives at home, although that is not always the case.

Child development experts say parents and caregivers can simply distract an infant from inappropriate behavior. "Distraction redirects curiosity; saying no discourages it," writes Burton L. White.[73] Yet parents and caregivers must begin to set clear limits on children's behavior as soon as possible, and follow through to see that the limits are obeyed. White suggests that parents and caregivers begin setting limits on children when they are between 7½ to 10 months of age.[74]

Research psychologists Leon Kuczynski and Grazyna Kochanska at the National Institute of Mental Health have found that the way a parent disciplines a child has a great effect on the child's developing conscience. Toddlers who are given clear limits, whose parents try to promote sympathy and compassion for others, and who are taught how to behave by being given instructions and explanations are more likely to comply with parents' requests than children who have been threatened or physically punished.[75] Parents of young children should keep lessons simple and positive, be ready to repeat simple rules, avoid using threats, and not expect young children to understand rules right away.

As children begin to interact with adults, peers, and situations outside the immediate family or primary care-giving environment, the issue of boundaries becomes more complex. As children develop, they are influenced more by what their peers are allowed to do and by what expectations are in settings beyond the home. When children are playing with other children in the neighborhood, they need to know the boundaries and expectations involved in playing with others and to understand the neighborhood or community areas that are "off limits." They need neighbors who keep an eye out for them and reinforce healthy boundaries. And as they enter other institutions in the community (such as schools, organizations, and religious congregations), they need to hear consistent messages about appropriate behavior, preferably similar to the messages they hear at home. Positive family communication is important in this respect: if open communication exists in the family, the child will feel able and safe to discuss conflicting messages.

▼ Asset No. 14: Adult role models

Children learn to behave and to interact with others by observing and imitating their parents, caregivers, and other adults—their displays of emotion, displays of affection, and interactions with others. Children thus need adults who set good examples and model positive, responsible behavior.

During infancy, many first-time parents wonder how to be an effective role model. "If parents do what comes naturally and provide a baby with generous amounts of love, attention, and physical care, nature will pretty much take care of the learning process," writes Burton L. White.[76] As children become more mobile as toddlers and preschoolers, however, adults must intentionally act in accord with what they teach. For example, parents should avoid kneeling or standing on counters to reach something on a top shelf when they are teaching their children not to climb on things that are not playground equipment.

Children's entry into school signals a change in the parent-child relationship. Although parental modeling continues to be essential, it becomes critically important that children have positive role models with the adults with whom they are spending more time. Teachers, coaches, and club leaders are among the nonfamily adults who set examples for how children act and talk. The more consistent messages children receive from all the adults in their lives, the better.

▼ Asset No. 15: Positive peer observations and interactions

In the same way that positive adult role models are important, so too are relationships with peers who model positive behavior. Although the characteristics of these relationships change over the course of childhood, considerable research has documented that close peer relationships are an essential part of social development during both childhood and adolescence. Children develop the foundation for these relationships early in life by developing skills for positive interaction with other children.

Even infants can learn a lot about peer interactions by observing their siblings and other children around them.[77] Children can learn to play well with others starting around age 18 months, but they should not be expected to share toys or to play with others for long periods of time. Toddlers and young preschool children interact with one another at varying levels of involvement, often engaging in "parallel play," playing side by side while doing different activities. As children reach the elementary school age years, they can learn to share, to empathize, and to understand that their behavior has consequences.

Probably the biggest influence on the way children play with other children is the relationship children have with their parents.[78] Researchers have suggested that this is because of either the interpersonal skills the child has learned from the interactions with the parent[79] or because the quality of the parent-child relationship influences the child's skills in getting along with others.[80]

Confirming the importance of parental influence on children's peer relationship skills, researcher Gary Ladd and his colleagues observed that mothers' disciplinary styles affected preschoolers' success in peer interactions. Children whose mothers encouraged them to have good judgment and who set limits and explained consequences to them were more likely to get along better with their peers than were children whose mothers' disciplinary styles involved hitting, yelling, and threatening.[81]

The behavior of preschoolers on the playground contributes to their social status among peers. Children who cooperate with their peers when on the playground tend to have more positive play relationships with peers.[83] Having positive peer relationships also predicts school adjustment. For example, in a study of more than 100 kindergartners, children who had a lot of friends in the classroom at the beginning of the school year developed positive perceptions of the school environment and had gains in school performance; conversely, kindergartners who were rejected by their peers early in the school year had more negative feelings about school and lower school performance during the entire school year.[84]

In general, children who are liked have good outcomes and children who are disliked are considered to be at risk for poor or negative outcomes. Willard W. Hartup of the Institute of Child Development at the University of Minnesota notes, however, that although having friends is an important part of development during childhood, the nature of the friendships also is important. "Supportive relationships between socially skilled individuals appear to be developmental advantages, whereas, coercive and conflict-ridden relationships are developmental disadvantages, especially among antisocial children."[85]

> "Discipline
> as we see it consists of
> living, loving, learning;
> of sharing and caring;
> of believing and trusting;
> but most of all
> of understanding."[82]
>
> Louise Bates Ames, Ph.D.
> Cofounder, Gesell Institute of
> Human Development

▼ Asset No. 16: Expectations for growth

Parents and caregivers should allow children to grow at their own pace and encourage them to develop their unique talents and do well. This requires parents and caregivers to understand basic information about child development, such as the different rates at which children grow. Parents' expectations and beliefs also influence children's development. As child psychology professor Jesus Palacios explains, "If a parent believes that a baby's vision does not develop until a certain age, the parent may not visually stimulate that baby, possibly delaying visual development."[86] Parental beliefs about whether their child's development or behavior is "off time" or "on time" also may affect the parents' attitudes about their parenting skills or the skills of their child.[87] Parents who are sensitive to child development issues and who are knowledgeable about parenting techniques are more apt to have realistic expectations and to bring out the best in their children.

	FIGURE 12		
	Boundaries-and-Expectations Assets through the Years		
	Infants and Toddlers (Birth to age 2)	**Preschoolers** (Ages 3 to 5)	**Elementary-Age Children** (Ages 6 to 11)
11.	**Family boundaries**		
	Parent(s) are aware of the child's preferences and adapt the environment to best suit the child's needs. Parent(s) begin setting limits as the child becomes mobile.	Family has clear rules and consequences. Family monitors the child and consistently demonstrates appropriate behavior through modeling and limit setting.	Family has clear rules and consequences, and monitors the child's whereabouts.
12.	**Out-of-home boundaries**		**School boundaries**
	Child care and other out-of-home environments have clear rules and consequences while consistently providing the child with appropriate stimulation and enough rest.	Neighbors, child care, preschool, and community provide clear rules and consequences.	School provides clear rules and consequences.
13.	**Neighborhood boundaries**		
	Neighbors take responsibility for monitoring child's behavior as the child begins to play and interact outside the home.		Neighbors take responsibility for monitoring the child's behavior.
14.	**Adult role models**		
	Parent(s) and other adults model positive, responsible behavior.		
15.	**Positive peer observation**	**Positive peer interactions**	**Positive peer interactions**
	Child observes positive peer interactions of siblings and other children and has opportunities for beginning interactions with children of various ages.	Child's interactions with other children are encouraged and promoted. Child is given opportunities to play with other children in a safe, well-supervised setting.	Child plays with children who model responsible behavior.
16.	**Expectations for growth**		
	Parent(s) are realistic in their expectations of development at this age. Parent(s) encourage development but do not push the child beyond his or her own pace.	Adults have realistic expectations of development at this age. Parent(s), caregivers, and other adults encourage child to achieve and develop his or her unique talents.	

	FIGURE 13
	Ways to Provide Boundaries for Children

Age	Practical age-appropriate ideas
0–1	• Understand that children at this age do not intentionally violate standards.
	• Distract children from inappropriate behavior and draw attention to appropriate behavior.
	• Encourage children to try new skills without pushing.
1–2	• Expose children to other children their age but do not expect them to play together.
	• Give simple, understandable boundaries, such as "Don't bite" or "Be quiet."
	• Enforce boundaries consistently so children learn them more easily.
3–5	• Demonstrate appropriate behaviors; do not just tell children what to do and what not to do.
	• Be calm when children act out in highly emotional ways.
	• Encourage children to play with one other child on a regular basis to learn social skills.
6–11	• Be firm about safety boundaries.
	• Encourage schools, families, and community organizations to have consistent boundaries and consequences.
	• Be consistent with the consequences for violating boundaries.

Chapter 6   Enriching Activities: The Constructive-Use-of-Time Assets

ow a child spends her or his time contributes greatly to development. Most young children, however, do not control how they spend their time; their parents and caregivers do. With many families feeling stressed because of having limited time and resources, children are more at risk than ever before for having too much unstructured, unsupervised time. More than two million children between the ages of 6 and 13 care for themselves during the after-school hours, with little or no parent or other adult supervision.[88] In his research on self-care or "latch-key" children, Temple University psychologist Laurence Steinberg found that children between the ages of 11 and 16 who were are not allowed to "hang out" and whose parents supervised them by telephone or by making sure chores were assigned to them were less likely to participate in risky behaviors in the after-school hours than were self-care children who were not supervised.[89]

Many school-age children have too few supervised, meaningful after-school opportunities. Some children, however, have too much structured time. Activities, clubs, and events jam their schedules from early morning to late evening. They lack time with their families, time with their friends, and time by themselves.

All children need a balance of structured and unstructured time. To ensure healthy development, they need time of sufficient frequency and quality with their families. And as they grow, children also need access to high-quality, affordable activities that build their competencies and expose them to caring adults beyond the family. These needs are reflected in the four constructive-use-of-time assets.

▼ Asset No. 17: Creative activities

Early and ongoing exposure to and participation in the arts—music, drama, painting, and so forth—can have a profound effect on children. Not only does this develop an appreciation for aesthetics, but it also can teach skills, build discipline (through regular practice), and enhance self-esteem, among other benefits.

Creative activities can begin at birth. Even infants respond to music. Newborns have been shown to increase their sucking in response to folk music and to attempt to avoid non-rhythmic noise.[90] Babies between the ages of four and six months even begin to "bounce" to music.[91] Researchers say that not only do the quality of play materials and daily experiences with music, art, and drama add pleasure to a child's life, but they also are predictors of achievement test scores in fourth and fifth grades.[92]

▼ Asset No. 18: Out-of-home activities

Childhood is a time of exploration, discovery, and learning. Children need opportunities to discover the world around them and their place in it through activities beyond the home. In addition, out-of-home activities become important opportunities to build social skills, form relationships with caring peers and adults, and develop personal interests. Infants need stimulating out-of-home activities, such as going to the grocery store, a concert in the park, or a walk at a zoo. Older children need supervised, structured activities that allow them to interact with children outside the home and that encourage them to grow and expand their social skills.

Out-of-home activities should be planned with the child's needs in mind and should be worthwhile for the child. Moreover, adults need to carefully monitor their child's response to stimulation and make adjustments, if necessary. For

---

FIGURE 14

Essential Keys to School-Age Child Care

What makes some out-of-home organizational settings better for children than others? Project KIDS, a school-age child care program at Rahn Elementary School in Eagan, Minn., says successful child care programs do five things. They:

1. **Empower children** with activities that allow them to develop, grow, and make decisions, instead of herding them physically from activity area to activity area on a schedule.

2. **Offer times of play** in which children learn the skills of playing hard, playing fair, and how to rest, instead of keeping children busy by having every minute planned by an adult.

3. **Plan community-building activities** that promote leadership sharing, caring behaviors, altruism, and friendships, instead of creating an activity-led program where activities are planned haphazardly without purpose.

4. **Promote maturity** by having older and wiser adults and youth help children grow socially, psychologically, and ethically, instead of emphasizing sophistication where children become street-smart by being exposed to situations beyond their comprehension.

5. **Encourage the development of self-discipline** so that children learn the skills of self-control and self-discipline, instead of being teacher-punished, meaning that children are oversupervised and have all decisions made for them.

Information from Laurie Ollhoff, *Giving Children Their Childhood Back* (St. Paul: Minnesota Department of Education, 1993), 3–21.

example, one two-year-old may find a three-hour visit to the zoo stimulating, while another may become overwhelmed by all the activity within an hour.

Important barriers may exist that prevent children from becoming involved in out-of-home activities. In a Search Institute study of structured, out-of-home opportunities for 7- to 14-year-olds in Minneapolis, young people surveyed cited participation barriers including transportation problems, lack of interest in available activities, and lack of knowledge about activities. In addition, one-third of these young people—and more than half of the parents surveyed—said that program costs were a barrier.[93] Parents said, too, that they were concerned about their children's safety getting to and from activities, and more than one-third also said they had fears about safety at the activities.[94]

▼ Asset No. 19: Religious community

Involvement in a religious community—church, synagogue, mosque, temple, or other faith community—promotes positive development because it exposes children to positive values and to positive relationship-building activities. Religious institutions are one of the major social contexts that intentionally

| | FIGURE 15 | | |
| | **Constructive-Use-of-Time Assets through the Years** | | |
	Infants and Toddlers (Birth to age 2)	**Preschoolers** (Ages 3 to 5)	**Elementary-Age Children** (Ages 6 to 11)
17.	**Creative activities**		
	Parent(s) daily expose the child to music, art, or other creative activities.	Child participates in music, art, or dramatic play on a daily basis.	Child participates in music, arts, or drama three or more hours each week through home and out-of-home activities.
18.	**Out-of-home activities**		**Child programs**
	Parent(s) expose the child to limited but stimulating situations outside of the home. Family attends events with the child's needs in mind.	Child interacts with children outside the family. Family attends events with the child's needs in mind.	Child spends one hour or more per week in extracurricular school activities or structured community programs.
19.	**Religious community**		
	Family attends religious programs or services on a regular basis while keeping the child's needs in mind.		Family attends religious programs or services for at least one hour per week.
20.	**Positive, supervised time at home**		
	Parent(s) supervise the child at all times and provide predictable and enjoyable routines at home.	Child is supervised by an adult at all times. Child spends most evenings and weekends at home with parent(s) in predictable, fun, enjoyable routines.	Child spends most evenings and weekends at home with parent(s) in predictable and enjoyable routines.

address moral development, which is an integral part of healthy development in adolescence and adulthood. A religious community is an important socializing system that can provide support for the values a family cherishes. Studies of families involved in congregations consistently find that the parent's religious values are strong predictors of the child's moral and religious values.[95]

While faith communities today tend to be as age-segregated as other sectors of U.S. society, congregations have the potential to be more intergenerational than most other institutions. Those congregations that realize this potential have a particular capacity to build assets for children. Congregations also typically offer a range of structured activities for children, such as religious education, community service projects, music, and informal activities that can build positive relationships and skills.[97]

Adults in religious congregations need to be aware of child development issues and keep children's needs in mind. Congregations that expect two-year-olds to sit still for an hour-long worship service are thinking more of the capacities of adults than of children. Ideally, all of the congregation's programs and experiences should be designed with the needs and interests of children in mind (including providing child care or other alternatives for children during adult-focused activities).

Little research exists on the impact of involvement in a religious community on a child's overall development from birth to age 11. In a review of the relation between religion and well-being in adolescence, however, Michael J. Donahue and Peter L. Benson found that religious involvement is positively related to prosocial values and behaviors and that it can reduce negative or risky behaviors, such as substance abuse, suicide, delinquency, and premature sexual involvement.[98] We believe that the positive impact of religious involvement on adolescents' healthy development would hold true for younger children.

▼ Asset No. 20: Positive, supervised time at home

Children need family time in order to feel cherished and protected. Young children should spend most of their evenings and weekends with their families. Although young children need some out-of-home activity and, as they grow, time to play with friends from the neighborhood and school, the majority of time should be spent at home. Child psychiatrist Stanley I. Greenspan says that parents should set aside unstructured "floor time" with their child each day, playing according to the child's wishes. "During this time, about 30 minutes a day at a minimum, you get down on the floor with your child, trying to 'march to your child's drummer,'" he says.[99]

While structured activity is essential for a child's development, a child also needs unstructured time to freely explore and play as she or he wishes. Too much activity overstimulates a child; too little activity understimulates a child. "Neither children nor adults should be expected to function at the utmost limits of their capacities every day, all day," says Lilian G. Katz, a professor of early childhood education at the University of Illinois, Urbana-Champaign. "We are all more likely to do well when there is a balance between our tasks and activities."[100]

Adult supervision is important for children at all ages. For children under the age of five, constant adult supervision ensures safety. Children in elementary school and middle school also need supervision even though they may appear independent. Most states have laws pertaining to adult supervision; many states require that children under a certain age be supervised. The American Academy of Pediatrics recommends that children 12 and younger should not be without adult (or responsible adolescent) supervision.[101]

hildren's time at home should not be dominated by the television set. Moreover, the quality and content of the programming children watch should be carefully monitored. Wendy Wood and her colleagues at Texas A & M University found that children who watched violent programs played more violently and aggressively than children who watched only nonviolent programming.[102] *The Position Statement on Media Violence in Children's Lives,* adopted by the National Association for the Education of Young Children, states that children are especially vulnerable to violent and negative programming because "up until age seven or eight, children have great difficulty distinguishing fantasy from reality, and their ability to comprehend nuances of behavior, motivation, or moral complexity is limited."[103]

Early exposure to television violence may predict aggression into adolescence or young adulthood. In a now classic study, researchers found that third-grade

FIGURE 16
Ways to Promote Constructive-Use-of-Time Assets

Age	Practical age-appropriate ideas
0–1	• Have babies and young children spend most of their time with their parents or one or two consistent caregivers.
	• Encourage adults to be flexible with a child's schedule and gradually introduce predictable routines.
	• Monitor stimulation at this age carefully, as children can easily become understimulated or overstimulated.
1–2	• Have consistent times for children to sleep, eat, play, and relax.
	• Balance stimulating, structured time with free playtime.
	• Encourage and equip parents to have positive, meaningful family times at home with their children.
3–5	• Encourage families to find simple household chores that family members can do together.
	• Follow children's lead in which activities interest them most and expose them to other related activities.
	• Introduce children to museums, children's plays, and other events that welcome young children.
6–11	• Teach children the skill of balancing their time so they gradually learn how not to overbook or underbook their schedules.
	• Allow children to have one or two out-of-the-home activities that are led by caring, nurturing adults.
	• Encourage families to have a family night at least once a month to do something fun together.

boys' preference for violent television programs was the strongest predictor of aggression when the boys became adolescents.[104] Parents can ameliorate the negative effects of television violence by helping children to evaluate the consequences and to discuss and find constructive alternatives to violence that they have watched on television.[105]

The Internal Assets

Chapters 7 through 10 focus on four categories of internal assets that need to be nurtured and developed within children over time, shaping children's character and commitments. Altogether there are 20 internal assets in four categories: commitment to learning, positive values, social competencies, and positive identity. Most of these assets are external in infancy and early childhood; they begin to be internalized by children during elementary school. They continue to develop during adolescence and young adulthood.

Chapter 7

A Foundation for Learning: The Commitment-to-Learning Assets

hildren are naturally curious. They love to explore, to learn, and to try new things. Yet many children's curiosity wanes and their desire to learn fades somewhere along their journey through childhood. One reason this may occur is that many adults do not have or take the time to teach and to encourage children—and to model the joy of learning. Moreover, often parents and teachers are seen as the only people who can influence a child's commitment to learning, thus reducing children's access to other positive role models and educational advocates in the community. Furthermore, societal influences often cast learning in a negative light or focus on extrinsic punishments and rewards (such as grades and prizes) that may preclude children's development of intrinsic motivation.[106]

"Children learn in every waking hour, wherever they are, whatever they are doing."[107]

Carnegie Task Force on Learning in the Primary Grades

Many adults also have the misconception that learning pertains only to academics. Everything about life involves learning, however. Curiosity and the motivation to learn aid children when they want to learn how to rollerblade, fold a paper airplane, or build a sand castle. Children who maintain their love of learning as they grow also certainly are more apt to learn many essential skills, such as cooking, car maintenance, and budgeting their money.

In September 1996, the Carnegie Task Force on Learning in the Primary Grades recommended five essential strategies to improve children's healthy development and learning between the ages of 3 and 10. These strategies are: promoting children's learning in families and communities; expanding high-quality early learning opportunities; creating effective elementary schools and school systems; promoting high-quality children's television and access to other electronic media; and linking the key learning institutions into a comprehensive, coordinated educational system.[108]

These strategies are important to help foster children's curiosity, encourage their learning, and instill in them a commitment to lifelong learning. Adults can begin by thinking of themselves as teachers, supporters, advocates, role models, and cheerleaders of children as they discover and internalize these values.

Within the category of commitment to learning are five assets. For infants, toddlers, and preschoolers (birth to age five), the assets focus more on what adults provide in an environment that encourages learning. For elementary-age children, the assets emphasize the development of an internal motivation for and commitment to learning.

▼ Asset No. 21: Achievement
▼ Asset No. 22: Engagement

The first two commitment-to-learning assets highlight the importance of school achievement and active engagement in learning. Adults who are responsive and attentive can set the stage for children becoming engaged in learning. Researcher Reginald M. Clark has found that poor black children who are high-achievers tend to live in homes where parents play a major role in the child's schooling, expect the children to continue education after high school, and provide a family life that is conducive to learning.[109] Researchers also have found that the motivation to achieve is related to the quality of the relationship between the infant and the parent. Infants with a secure attachment to their mothers are more likely to feel safe to leave their mother's side and explore.[110]

The motivation to achieve is related to taking pride in one's own ability and feeling a sense of self-fulfillment.[111] Researcher Susan Harter suggests that children strive to achieve either to satisfy their own needs (intrinsic motivation) or as a means to earn incentives such as grades and rewards (extrinsic motivation).[112] She observed that intrinsically motivated children prefer challenging tasks and view themselves as more competent than do extrinsically motivated children. Furthermore, children who are intrinsically motivated are more likely to develop self-starting skills that enhance their growth in all areas, whether they are playing, learning a new skill, or doing school work.

▼ Asset No. 23: Stimulating activity and homework

Stimulation for learning and opportunities for learning on one's own also are important for developing a commitment to learning.

Infants learn mainly by smelling, looking, listening, and touching. During early infancy, babies can discriminate black-and-white and colors and a variety of patterns, and early stimulation is critical to learning later in life.[113] One study showed that children with the highest motivation to achieve had parents who provided sensory stimulation aimed at amusing children and arousing their curiosity as infants.[114] Although activities involving looking, listening, and touching are important, parents should pay attention to the baby's response to stimulation. Babies respond best to interactions when they are calm and alert. They will then take an active part in interaction with the caregiver, which can be observed in the way they wave their arms and legs, gurgle, gaze intently, and smile.[115] When an infant turns away or fusses, however, this indicates that the level of stimulation should be changed. An infant might be over-stimulated and need to have the stimulation moderated, or an infant may need more stimulation.

Many researchers and practitioners have suggested that the amount and quality of stimulation in children's early home and caregiving environments will affect later achievement and even IQ scores.[116] Recent research on children in Romanian

FIGURE 17		
Commitment-to-Learning Assets through the Years		
Infants and Toddlers (Birth to age 2)	**Preschoolers** (Ages 3 to 5)	**Elementary-Age Children** (Ages 6 to 11)
21. **Achievement expectation**		**Achievement motivation**
Family members are motivated to do well at work, school, and in the community, and model this to the child.	Parent(s) and other adults convey and reinforce expectations to do well at work, school, in the community, and within the family.	Child is motivated to do well in school.
22. **Engagement expectation**		**School engagement**
The family models responsive and attentive attitudes at work, school, in the community, and at home.		Child is responsive, attentive, and actively engaged in learning.
23. **Stimulating activity**		**Homework**
Parent(s) encourage the child to explore and provide stimulating toys that match the child's emerging skills. Parent(s) are sensitive to the child's level of development and tolerance for movement, sounds, and duration of activity.	Parent(s) and other adults encourage the child to explore and provide stimulating toys that match the child's emerging skills. Parent(s) and other adults are sensitive to the child's level of development.	Child does homework when it is assigned.
24. **Enjoyment of learning**		**Bonding to school**
Parent(s) enjoy learning, and demonstrate this through their own learning activities.	Parent(s) and other adults enjoy learning and engage the child in learning activities.	Child cares about her or his school.
25. **Reading for pleasure**		
Parent(s) read to the child daily in enjoyable ways.	Caring adult(s) read to the child for at least 30 minutes a day.	Child and a caring adult read together for at least 30 minutes a day. Child also enjoys reading without an adult's involvement.

orphanages has shown that the length of time that infants were exposed to unstimulating environments was directly related to delays in their development of fine motor skills, gross motor skills, and language.[117] Recovery may be possible for the children, who suffered extreme lack of stimulation as well as inadequate nutrition and care before being adopted by British and American families, but researcher Michael Rutter cautions that experts would need to follow these children over the course of their growing-up years to completely understand the effect of the deprivation.[118]

arental involvement in play (such as the parent talking or otherwise interacting with the child and the parent structuring children's play periods) and high-quality play materials (such as age-appropriate toys) during infancy and preschool are strong predictors of achievement in the fourth and fifth grades.[119] And in a longitudinal study of 112 mothers and their two- to four-year-old children, researcher Keith Yeates and his colleagues found that the quality of stimulation in the home was a strong predictor of IQ scores when the children were four years old.[120]

As toddlers, children continue to need their learning abilities and imaginations stimulated. Young children learn mainly through experiences—hearing, seeing, touching, tasting, and smelling. Parents and caregivers can provide a variety of stimulating activity, but they also need to step back and allow children to explore and learn, says Richard Roberts of Utah State University.[121] Parents, caregivers, and teachers should be involved in children's play by struc-

	FIGURE 18
	Ways to Encourage a Commitment to Learning

Age	Practical age-appropriate ideas
0–1	• Sing and read to babies and toddlers daily.
	• Expose babies and toddlers to new environments, such as parks and stores.
	• Give new, interesting things to babies and toddlers to look at, such as toys in different colors, shapes, and sizes.
1–2	• Make a game for children to learn names of objects.
	• Help children group objects according to similarities.
	• Talk about what you see whenever you are with a child and ask the child to talk about what he or she sees.
3–5	• Encourage children to learn more about their interests.
	• Make up new songs, stories, and games to play with children.
	• Visit libraries, zoos, museums.
6–11	• Let children read to you every day as they learn to read.
	• Encourage families to set up a place for their children to do homework and set daily homework guidelines.
	• Visit new places with children to expose them to different cultures, people, and experiences.

FIGURE 19

Steps to the Long-Term Success of Learning

"The years from 3 to 10 are a crucial age span in a young person's life when a firm foundation is laid for healthy development and lifelong learning," says the Carnegie Task Force on Learning in the Primary Grades. The factors that foster lifelong learning are:

◆ A high-quality preschool or child care program that prepares children to enter elementary school.

◆ An elementary school that sets high learning standards.

◆ Parents who create a home environment that fosters learning.

◆ Parents who remain involved in their child's education.

◆ Communities that provide supportive programs for parents.

◆ Communities that offer out-of-school learning opportunities.

Information from the Carnegie Task Force on Learning in the Primary Grades, *Years of Promise: A Comprehensive Learning Strategy for America's Children* (New York: Carnegie Corporation of New York, 1996), vii.

---

turing the environment, setting limits and boundaries, and providing materials. Once a child has begun to play, however, adults should let children improvise, explore, and think. Nonetheless, adults need to monitor the play environment and to be available if the child needs and calls for assistance.

Children who do homework are more likely to grow up to be motivated, responsible adults.[122] Parents help support the development of responsibility by helping a child set up a homework area and develop a homework routine, and by assisting with assignments when the child needs this.[123] Teachers can help by assigning homework designed to enrich learning, not just to give children something they have to do.

▼ Asset No. 24: Enjoyment of learning and bonding to school

As important as the actual involvement in learning is the emotional climate or bond that helps children form a positive attachment to learning and places of learning. Too often, negative perceptions of schools and other learning institutions (such as libraries) by parents and others can inhibit children's learning and reduce their learning opportunities.

Families who enjoy learning are apt to expose babies and children to a diverse array of learning activities. Even infants can be taken to museums; many children's museums now have activities especially for toddlers. When their curiosity is fostered, children gradually begin to integrate new learning experiences into their everyday experience and to view learning environments in a positive light. When children begin elementary school, this interest in learning will help them bond to, or become invested in, school—which helps them identify with the goals of learning and appropriate behavior. It is not enough that children gain knowledge and skills in school. Bonding to school is a particularly important factor for promoting school success and academic achievement.[124]

▼ Asset No. 25: Reading for pleasure

Adults should read to infants from the day they are born. Although the infant does not understand the words, the sound and intonation of the parent or caregiver's voice is soothing and stimulating. Parents and caregivers can read parts of the daily newspaper aloud, parts of a novel, or even simple children's stories.

Reading to children, even from infancy, has been shown to have a number of positive effects on later outcomes. For example, one study of two-year-olds focused on when mothers began reading to their children, the frequency of reading, the number of stories they read, and how often the children visited a local library. The researchers observed that picture-book reading to young children was related to their development of receptive language (their understanding of what is being said). In addition, those children whose mothers began reading to them early were more likely to develop oral language skills earlier.[125]

Reading to young children also may help children adjust to their school environment. One study found that children's literature that portrayed positive and negative aspects of school could help young children deal with new classroom experiences and peer group relationships.[126]

While cloth books, board books, nursery rhymes, songbooks, finger games, and lullabies are ideal for infants, toddlers thrive on animal books, naming books, and stories with large, realistic pictures. As children enter the preschool years, books that whet their curiosity, help them with relationships, and deal with issues of power, fear, and independence will keep them interested in reading. Preschool children also can take trips to the library and help parents choose books for them. For six- and seven-year old children, their ability to understand stories will exceed their developing reading skills. To ensure children's continued interest in reading, parents and teachers must continue to read to young elementary-age children and must allow children to practice reading aloud as well.[127]

For eight- and nine-year-olds, reading needs to be further encouraged. Children at this age have many other competing interests, such as television, after-school activities, and friendships. Children at this age are becoming more independent readers, but they still enjoy being read to. By age 10 and 11, many children become absorbed in series books, such as Hardy Boys or Nancy Drew mysteries.[128] Any type of reading, including magazines or comic books, can be helpful.

In 1995, as part of its READ*WRITE*NOW! initiative, the U.S. Department of Education suggested children be read to or read with for at least 30 minutes a day.[129] This recommendation does not imply that infants, toddlers, and preschoolers can sit for 30 minutes straight and listen to a story. Reading experts suggest reading to children for a few minutes at a time over the course of a day, and that these reading intervals add up to 30 minutes. For example, parents may read labels aloud at the grocery store when their children are along. They can sing lullabies and nursery rhymes to young children, or read a story aloud while making faces and varying the tone of their voice to fit the story's characters. What is important is to make reading an enjoyable experience for the child. Says reading expert Jim Trelease, "Every time we read aloud to a child or class, we're giving a commercial for the pleasures of reading."[130]

Chapter 8   The Things We Stand For: The Positive-Values Assets

alues encompass our attitudes, our beliefs, and the standards for our actions. Values are the important "internal compasses" that guide people in developing priorities and making choices. Although the internalization of values takes place over time, the groundwork is laid from the first day of life. This chapter identifies six positive-values assets.

The first two values focus on caring for others, while the other four— integrity, honesty, responsibility, and restraint—focus more on personal character. The foundation of character building begins during infancy and slowly evolves through childhood and adolescence, all the while becoming more sophisticated and complex. People do not suddenly become honest and responsible when they become teenagers or adults. The development of these values is a long process that entails many interactions between children and adults.

Intentionally nurturing positive values in children is essential for parents, other caregivers, and child-serving institutions. Through the media, advertising, and popular culture, today's children are exposed to a barrage of messages that can shape their behaviors. While some of those messages are positive, many promote (intentionally or unintentionally) negative values such as self-centeredness, materialism, violence, and immediate gratification.

▼ Asset No. 26: Caring
▼ Asset No. 27: Equality and social justice

Developing a commitment to caring for others is an important developmental task. The well-being of society rests on all people knowing how and when to suspend their own personal gain to help the welfare of others. Although infants and toddlers are not developmentally capable of altruism, demonstrated family commitment to helping others—as well as the care given to the child—lays the groundwork for instilling caring in young children. Toddlers are capable of sympathy, which is a likely precursor to altruism. Toddlers will offer a toy to a companion, help with household chores,[131] or demonstrate compassion by trying to cheer up a distressed playmate. During the preschool and school-age years, families can get children involved in hands-on projects to help others.[132]

Research has shown that parental warmth and affection enhance the development of altruism in children,[133] and that children will imitate adults who model prosocial acts, such as honesty, generosity, helpfulness, or rescue.[134] Younger children may lack the role-taking ability necessary to completely understand the pain of others, however;[135] the ability to be truly empathic develops during adolescence and early adulthood.

Families who place a high value on equality, reducing poverty and hunger, and other social justice concerns are more likely to expose their children—even in early childhood—to these values. In families that value equality, for example, each family member is likely to be treated fairly, while families who do not prize equality may place a greater emphasis on adults than on children. As children enter the school-age years, families can expand their modeling of equality and social justice values to include care for strangers in the community and around the world. Participating in recycling projects, collecting items for a food shelf, and serving a meal to people who are homeless are all ways children can develop equality and social justice values.

▼ Asset No. 28: Integrity
▼ Asset No. 29: Honesty
▼ Asset No. 30: Responsibility

Integrity, honesty, and responsibility are three values assets that protect young people from engaging in risky behaviors and that increase the likelihood of positive outcomes, such as school success.[136]

Stephen L. Carter, the William Nelson Cromwell Professor of Law at Yale University, defines people with integrity as those who have a sense of moral reflectiveness, who keep their commitments, and who are unashamed of doing the right thing.[137] Parents and caregivers who demonstrate integrity by acting on their convictions and standing up for their beliefs model this behavior for their children. Young children develop integrity slowly through many repeated exposures to such modeling.

Honesty, too, is a value children learn by being exposed to adult modeling beginning in early childhood. Young children tend to make decisions impulsively based on immediate gratification. For example, a child sneaking cookies may find it easier to lie (or even to blame another child) in response to an inquiry because he or she fears getting caught. As parents and caregivers model honesty,

FIGURE 20

Moral Development in Children

During infancy, the foundation for moral development is laid by parents who are committed to positive values and who model those values by acting on them. By age three, children begin to be capable of feeling hurt, shame, guilt, empathy, pride, and need for reparation. By the elementary-school years, children who are more likely to begin to internalize values are those whose parents are concerned about others and who give children complex explanations of values and moral issues.

Information from Robert N. Emde, Zynep Biringen, Robert B. Clyman, and David Oppenheim, "The Moral Self of Infancy: Affective Core and Procedural Knowledge," *Developmental Review* 11 (1991): 251–70; Laurence J. Walker and John H. Taylor, "Family Interactions and the Development of Moral Reasoning," *Child Development* 62 (1991):264–83; and Carolyn U. Shanz, "Social Cognition," in *Handbook of Child Psychology*, vol. 3, ed. John H. Flavell and Ellen M. Markman (New York: Wiley, 1983), 495–555.

they need to be patient with children's impulsive actions, which are self-protective in nature. "Constant nurturing is needed to establish the thinking skills necessary to overcome strong impulses," writes educator Harlan S. Hansen.[138] Hansen suggests that parents and teachers encourage children to think about their actions and to understand what they are capable of doing rather than just spontaneously acting.

Adults also need to model honesty and to admit when they have been dishonest. Adults who admit to a child when they have been dishonest, explain why, and apologize set a good example of how to behave honestly and respectfully. Adults also can provide experiences and activities to help children learn and practice honesty in the controlled setting of the home, child care setting, and school so that children will know how to act even when they are not with their parents, caregivers, and teachers.[139]

Children learn the value of responsibility early in their lives as they find that their behavior affects other people. An infant can detect that smiling prompts others to smile back. Toddlers who throw their blocks may not be able to understand that this is unacceptable behavior, but they easily can see how a playmate reacts when getting hit with a block.

Parental monitoring is an important component of developing responsibility. Permissive parenting or a lack of parental monitoring is strongly associated with adolescent delinquency.[140] In addition to parental monitoring, parents and adults need to give children meaningful, age-appropriate activities to enhance personal responsibility. As children are able, they can begin to contribute to age-appropriate household tasks, such as cleaning their rooms, setting the table, or emptying wastebaskets. Children may need to "grow into" taking full responsibility for a task or project; at first they may only be parents' helpers. For example, a two-year-old would be overwhelmed with the sole responsibility of keeping his or her room clean unless the parent were to work side-by-side with the child. As the child grows older and can handle more responsibility, the parent can gradually shift responsibility to the child.[141]

▼ Asset No. 31: Healthy lifestyle and sexual attitudes

One of the key values for adolescents is restraint—the internal beliefs that keep them from engaging in risky or unhealthy behaviors such as early sexual activity and alcohol and other drug use. Children gradually develop the foundation for adolescent restraint by living in an environment that nurtures and encourages a healthy lifestyle and a healthy understanding of sexuality. Research confirms that adolescents are more likely to refrain from early sexual intercourse and alcohol or other drug use if they have been raised in an environment that promotes a healthy lifestyle.[142]

The way parents and caregivers touch, hold, and handle a child all lay the foundation for the child's development of healthy sexual attitudes and beliefs. Also relevant are parents' and caregivers' own views, beliefs, and values about sexuality. Clarifying sexual values is as important as giving children accurate information about sex, says professor of psychology Anne C. Bernstein.[143]

An important part of early sexuality education is parents' acceptance and encouragement of children's questions about sex. Parents' open discussion of sexual issues can contribute both to the formation of healthy values and the development of critical thinking and decision making skills.[144]

Children also need to be exposed to other aspects of a healthy lifestyle. Encouraging healthy habits in children can have lifetime benefits. The American Academy of Pediatrics says that adult eating preferences are developed during the second year of a child's life.[146] Parents and caregivers also need to help children develop good habits of sleeping, relaxation, and physical activity. Children need to get adequate sleep each night, and they also need to learn effective techniques for dealing with stress, such as talking with a caring adult, problem-solving, or distraction.

FIGURE 21
Ways to Nurture Positive Values

Age	Practical age-appropriate ideas
0–1	• Respond to children's cries immediately. • Create caring atmospheres at home, child care centers, nurseries, and other places for young children. • Encourage families to articulate their values while modeling and teaching them as their children grow.
1–2	• Show children how to act when they act inappropriately. • Find simple ways for children to care for others, such as giving hugs. • Interact with children in loving, respectful, and caring ways.
3–5	• Encourage parents to simply explain their values to children when they see others behaving in ways they value or do not value. • Affirm children's appropriate behavior. • Teach children how to care for a special toy, outfit, pet, or plant, but do not let children care for pets entirely by themselves.
6–11	• Encourage families to participate in service activities together. • Have children write thank-you notes or show their appreciation in some other way whenever they receive gifts. • Answer accurately and simply children's questions about sexuality, and about alcohol and other drugs. Ask if they would like more information and respect their answers.

FIGURE 22

Positive-Values Assets through the Years

	Infants and Toddlers (Birth to age 2)	Preschoolers (Ages 3 to 5)	Elementary-Age Children (Ages 6 to 11)
26.	**Family values caring**		**Caring**
	Parent(s) convey their beliefs about helping others by modeling helping behaviors.	Child is encouraged to express sympathy for someone who is distressed and to share her or his possessions with others.	Child is encouraged to help other people and to share her or his possessions with others.
27.	**Family values equality and social justice**		**Equality and social justice**
	Parent(s) place a high value on promoting equality and reducing hunger and poverty, and model these beliefs.		Child begins to show interest in making the community a better place.
28.	**Family values integrity**		**Integrity**
	Parent(s) act on convictions and stand up for their beliefs, and communicate and model this in the family.		Child begins to act on convictions and stand up for his or her beliefs.
29.	**Family values honesty**		**Honesty**
	Parent(s) tell the truth and convey their belief in honesty through their actions.	Child learns the difference between truth and lying.	Child begins to value honesty and act accordingly.
30.	**Family values responsibility**		**Responsibility**
	Parent(s) accept and take personal responsibility.	Child learns that actions have an effect on other people.	Child begins to accept and take personal responsibility for age-appropriate tasks.
31.	**Family values healthy lifestyle and sexual attitudes**		**Healthy lifestyle and sexual attitudes**
	Parent(s) love the child, setting the foundation for the child to develop healthy sexual attitudes and beliefs. Parent(s) model, monitor, and teach the importance of good health habits, such as providing good nutritional choices and adequate rest and play time.	Parent(s) and other adults model, monitor, and teach the importance of good health habits. Child learns healthy sexual attitudes and beliefs and to respect others.	Child begins to value good health habits. Child learns healthy sexual attitudes and beliefs and to respect others.

Chapter 9   Skills for Life: The Social-Competencies Assets

 s children encounter problems and life situations, social competencies help them cope with problems and move forward. Social competence involves the personal skills children develop to deal with the many choices, challenges, and opportunities they face in life. The skills identified in the asset framework include planning and decision-making, interpersonal and cultural competencies, resistance, and peaceful conflict resolution.

Building social competence is a slow process and occurs over time. Even exceptionally talented individuals develop their skills slowly, with a lot of practice. An Olympic diver does not acquire her or his skills within a few months—or even within a few years.

Children's development of social competence is affected by interactions with their environment.[147] During infancy, children learn social skills through observation, taking in information by observing the people around them. Toddlers begin to experiment by talking and doing. As children progress through the preschool and elementary-school years, they expand their social competencies through more in-depth discussions and by practicing more complex tasks.

▼ Asset No. 32: Planning and decision-making

Planning and decision-making skills are essential for success. These skills need to be nurtured early in life and reinforced, strengthened, and deepened over time.

Parents and caregivers can demonstrate and teach planning and decision-making skills to older babies and toddlers by giving them simple choices, such as between apple or orange juice or in planning what to wear. Children make better decisions when they have had practice. Researcher Lisa Freund at Johns Hopkins University School of Medicine found that three- to five-year-old children solved problems better if they had worked previously on a similar problem with a parent.[148]

As children enter school, their opportunities for planning and decision-making increase and become more complex. Involving children in more and more decisions that affect them not only builds skills, but it also increases children's sense of empowerment and competence.

The ability to solve problems creatively is an important component of planning and decision-making skills. Creativity helps children realize that there are many possibilities in life and many different ways of seeing the world. People are more likely to have creative abilities as adults "if they develop the skill and the motivation for creativity as children," writes Teresa M. Amabile in *Growing Up Creative*.[149] Amabile's research on the importance of developing creativity as well as intrinsic motivation in children suggests that "in helping children to become their most creative selves, it is not enough for us to train them in skills or give them opportunities in which to develop their talents.... We must help them identify the places where their interests and their skills overlap."[150]

▼ Asset No. 33: Interpersonal skills

Infants and toddlers learn social skills by being with family members who love, care for, and play with them. But developing skill in interacting with people takes years and years of practice. While one-to-one interactions are important, so are group social situations. "Successful involvement in group play helps to foster self-esteem—and this social 'training' helps to set the stage for how children will relate to others as adults," says Joal Hetherington, a writer who specializes in children's issues.[151] Parents and caregivers can model interpersonal skills by the way they greet people, talk, and interact with others.

Children's ability to think about themselves and their relationships with other people is something that develops gradually and is related to their level of cognitive development. Psychologist Robert Selman suggests that this has to do with the development of role-taking skills, the ability to distinguish one's own perspective from that of a companion.[152]

The ability to express emotion also is important in interpersonal skills. In *Emotional Intelligence*, Daniel Goleman contends that being able to manage emotions is critical to success in life.[154] From early on, children should be encouraged to express feelings, and family members should be interested in their feelings and thoughts. Parents and caregivers can help develop these interpersonal skills by teaching children how to express their feelings in words rather than actions.

Once children are in preschool and elementary school, they begin to develop the intellectual capacity to articulate their feelings, rework past emotional situations verbally through play, reflect on feelings, and understand the perspectives or feelings of others. Researcher Judy Dunn and her colleagues found

"What children need to learn is how to go about acquiring new skills to meet contemporary problems or older problems seen from a new point of view."[153]

Margaret Mead
Anthropologist

that families who expressed and described their feelings raised children who were more likely to identify their own feelings and who were more skilled at reading the feelings of others, a crucial social skill.[155]

	FIGURE 23		
	Social-Competencies Assets through the Years		
	Infants and Toddlers (Birth to age 2)	**Preschoolers** (Ages 3 to 5)	**Elementary-Age Children** (Ages 6 to 11)
32.	**Planning and decision-making observation**	**Planning and decision-making practice**	**Planning and decision-making**
	Parent(s) make all safety and care decisions for the child and model these behaviors. Parent(s) allow the child to make simple choices as the child becomes more independently mobile.	Child begins to make simple choices, solve simple problems, and develop simple plans at an age-appropriate level.	Child learns beginning skills of how to plan ahead and makes decisions at an appropriate developmental level.
33.	**Interpersonal observation**	**Interpersonal interactions**	**Interpersonal competence**
	Parent(s) model positive and constructive interactions with other people. Parent(s) accept and are responsive to the child's expression of feelings, interpreting those expressions as cues to the child's needs.	Child plays and interacts with other children and adults. Child freely expresses feelings and is taught to articulate feelings verbally. Parent(s) and other adults model and teach empathy.	Child interacts with adults and children and can make friends. Child expresses and articulates feelings in appropriate ways and empathizes with others.
34.	**Cultural observation**	**Cultural interactions**	**Cultural competence**
	Parent(s) have knowledge of and are comfortable with people of different cultural/racial/ethnic backgrounds, and model this to the child.	Child is positively exposed to knowledge and people of different cultural/racial/ethnic backgrounds.	Child has knowledge of and comfort with people of different cultural/racial/ethnic backgrounds.
35.	**Resistance observation**	**Resistance practice**	**Resistance skills**
	Parent(s) model resistance skills by their own behaviors. Parent(s) are not overwhelmed by the child's needs and thereby demonstrate appropriate resistance skills.	Child is taught to resist participating in behavior that is inappropriate or dangerous.	Child begins to develop the ability to resist negative peer pressure and dangerous situations.
36.	**Peaceful conflict resolution observation**	**Peaceful conflict resolution practice**	**Peaceful conflict resolution**
	Parent(s) behave in acceptable, nonviolent ways and assist the child to develop these skills when faced with challenging or frustrating circumstances by helping child solve problems.	Parent(s) and other adults model peaceful conflict resolution. Child is taught and begins to practice nonviolent, acceptable ways deal with challenging and frustrating situations.	Child attempts to resolve conflict nonviolently.

▼ Asset No. 34: Cultural competence

We define cultural competence as knowing and being comfortable with people of different ethnic and racial backgrounds, valuing ethnic and racial differences, and respecting others' values and beliefs.[156]

Ideally, children should be raised by adults who know and are comfortable with people of different ethnic and racial backgrounds. Adults would then expose children to people and customs of various cultures and form strong, caring relationships with a diverse group of people. In reality, however, even parents who value diversity may find themselves struggling with how to teach their children culturally competent skills and values.

To develop a sense of cultural competence, children first develop an ethnic awareness and a cultural identity of their own. Frances Aboud, professor of psychology at McGill University in Montreal has done extensive research on the relation between ethnic awareness and prejudice.[157] Aboud reports that between the ages of six and eight, children begin to develop an awareness of the differences and similarities among people of other races. Children of differing ethnic groups vary in the ways they perceive themselves and people of other groups. Aboud found that children of color are more likely than are white children to react more negatively toward people of their own ethnic groups than to people of other groups.[158]

Other researchers have speculated that children of color mirror the negative images they receive in white-majority cultures. In their research on African American children in the United States, Darlene Powell Hopson and Derek Hopson write, "The danger is that Black children will identify with, or see themselves in the negative images of Blacks mirrored back to them by society." They say that African American children who are raised with open acknowledgment of racial issues in our society, who have positive black role models, and who receive positive reinforcement about being African American are more likely than are children without these influences to have high self-esteem and strong, positive ethnic awareness and identity.[159]

Ethnic awareness precedes prejudice, but it does not *determine* prejudice.[160] Aboud believes prejudice may be related to the way conflicts are handled within the family. "Prejudiced people tended to have parents who, to enhance or maintain their own social status, imposed rigid conventional rules of conduct on their children," she says. "Because of their parents' punitiveness, prejudiced people never learn to express hostility to their parents or to authority figures. Instead they displace this hostility on to people who lack authority and power, that is on to minority groups." Aboud also says that "unprejudiced people tended to have parents who accepted their individual qualities and

---

FIGURE 24

Interpersonal Success

"Childhood and adolescence are critical windows of opportunity for setting down the essential emotional habits that will govern our lives," writes Daniel Goleman in *Emotional Intelligence*. Goleman suggests three keys to interpersonal success:

1. Self-monitoring the expression of one's emotions.

2. Being keenly attuned to the way others react.

3. Adjusting the way one acts with others to ensure it has the desired effect on the other person.

Information from Daniel Goleman, *Emotional Intelligence* (New York: Bantam, 1995), xiii, 119.

---

who helped them express their aggression openly in modified and controlled ways. Such people learned to express hostility toward parents or other authority figures in an appropriate way."[161]

▼ Asset No. 35: Resistance skills

Children who have resistance skills and can say "no" or resist participating in a behavior that they have been taught is unacceptable or dangerous are more likely to grow up healthy than are children without these skills. Resistance skills have become an important ingredient in alcohol and other drug prevention programs.[162]

Having a healthy identity is a precursor for a child's development of resistance skills. The formation of a healthy identity begins in infancy by a parent's reflecting back—or "mirroring"—to the infant the sounds, postures, and expressions that the parent senses the child is experiencing.[163] "The infant and child use others as models, mirrors and relationships," writes physician Charles L. Whitfield. "If these are unhealthy, the infant and child get a distorted view of themselves and others."[164]

Teaching children resistance skills also involves teaching them how to set their own healthy boundaries. Between the ages of one and three, the child tests herself or himself, others, and the world to learn what the boundaries are. For example, the toddler will repeatedly do something the parent has said "no" to; often parents perceive this as the child's way of testing whether the parent actually means "no." By ages four or five, the child begins to model his or her behavior after that of parents and other caregiving adults. Careful parental modeling and guidance can teach children to avoid behavior that is inappropriate or dangerous. For example, parents who model excessive use of alcohol, tobacco, or other drugs may be signaling that this is acceptable behavior.

Once the child enters school, she or he begins to be cognitively more able to resist dangerous situations without the constant aid of an adult. The child slowly internalizes the ability to resist danger through repeated exposure to situations that require choices, as well as through repeated lessons from parents on how to handle situations. The parent's self-control and judgment become part of the child's own set of emotional and cognitive skills. What used to require an adult's presence now can be accomplished by the child alone by making use of these internalized capabilities.[165] The development of resistance skills takes a lot of practice. Each time the child says "no," she or he becomes more capable of resisting more complex pressures later in life.[166] Conversations with adults about these experiences also help to teach this skill.

▼ Asset No. 36: Peaceful conflict resolution

Conflict-resolution skills are difficult to master, and many adults have yet to do so. "Aggressive urges come out of a positive developmental impulse," says educator J. Ronald Lally. "Learning to assert him- or herself is essential to [a] child's development of a strong sense of self."[167] One key to a child's development of conflict resolution skills lies in how the parent or caregiver responds to the child's early expressions of violence or aggression. Withdrawing from a biting baby and redirecting the behavior of toddlers are good strategies to set the stage for conflict resolution skills. As the child grows, adults need to model and to teach peaceful ways to resolve conflicts, such as talking about issues after emotions have simmered down. Ensuring that children have adequate play space also is important; this will help to reduce accidental shoves, tripping, and bumping among children that some—especially young children—could misinterpret as intentional.[168]

In observing how family members interacted when there is at least one highly aggressive child in the home, researcher Gerald R. Patterson found that these children were growing up in families who displayed little affection and a lot of tension.[169] He calls this type of family atmosphere a "coercive family environment" because a great deal of the interactions among family members involve one family member trying to force or coerce another family member into changing his or her behavior. Patterson found that the parents of aggressive children rarely used positive parenting techniques, such as approval, as a means of controlling behavior. Instead, these parents tended to ignore the "good" things their children did, relying instead on coercive tactics, or force, to deal with their children's misconduct. Children from noncoercive families received much more positive attention.[170] Clearly, these behaviors are part of a family *system*, in which both children and parents are influencing each other's behavior.

FIGURE 25

Dealing with Conflict

What are some ways of dealing with children who are "out of control?" Researcher Gerald R. Patterson suggests:

♦ Do not give in to the child's unacceptable behavior.

♦ Do not exploit the child by trying to be more coercive than the child.

♦ Use the disciplinary technique of a time-out. Send the child to a specific place (such as a chair or a corner) until he or she calms down and changes behavior. Do not send the child to her or his room or a play area since the child may think he or she is getting rewarded, not punished.

♦ Identify the most irritating behaviors of the child and clearly point out those behaviors. Establish a system for earning "credit" (such as specific rewards or privileges) for appropriate behavior. Explain to the child how she or he loses credit for inappropriate behavior. Then follow through with this system consistently.

Information from Gerald R. Patterson, *Coercive Family Processes* (Eugene, Ore.: Castilia Press, 1982).

	FIGURE 26
	Ways to Promote Social Competencies

Age	Practical age-appropriate ideas
0–1	• Encourage children to experiment with sounds and in touching new things.
	• Affirm children as they learn new skills.
	• Expose children to new foods as they start to eat solids.
1–2	• Allow children to express all feelings, but give them guidelines on appropriate and inappropriate ways to act on them.
	• Give children at least two equally appealing choices whenever possible.
	• Arrange to have children play near another child who is around the same age.
3–5	• Emphasize the concept of sharing. Model sharing whenever possible.
	• Continue to cheer on children's new skills, such as cutting, drawing, walking backward, and so on.
	• Encourage families to start having periodic family meetings where children have input and a voice in decision-making.
6–11	• Allow children opportunities to succeed and fail.
	• Encourage children to develop more skills in areas in which they are interested.
	• Emphasize children should use words—rather than actions—to articulate their needs.

Chapter 10   Knowing Who We Are: The Positive-Identity Assets

Forging an individual identity is a lifelong process, but one that starts in infancy.[171] To form a positive identity, children need love and support. They also need to know and to understand their limits and boundaries and to feel empowered. Children also are more likely to develop positive self-images when they enjoy learning, find their activities stimulating and enriching, acquire positive values, and develop social competencies. Thus, many of the other assets play a part in building a positive identity.

How others respond to the child also greatly affects the child's identity. Children who are given clear, logical boundaries that are enforced consistently and with sensitivity are more likely to feel loved and capable, which in turn affects how they interact with other people. Children who feel loved and supported unconditionally are more apt to feel secure enough to take appropriate risks and to learn. These children are more likely to grow into competent, healthy, and productive adults.

The assets framework identifies four elements of positive identity: personal power, self-esteem, sense of purpose, and positive view of personal future.

▼ Asset No. 37: Personal power

A sense of personal control and power is critical for positive identity. People who do not have a sense that they have power over the things that happen to them can feel helpless, passive, and victimized.

A sense of personal control for children begins with their parents or caregivers. Parents who believe they control things that happen to them tend to feel empowered and to have a strong sense of identity. They model and teach self-management skills to their children.

Even at a young age, children begin developing a sense of personal power—or the belief that they do not have any. The only muscles a newborn voluntarily can control are those used for eye movement and for sucking. During the next three months of life, the infant slowly gains rudimentary control of his or her arms and legs. Gradually the flailing arms become reaching arms. Then crawling, walking, and talking occur; each of these significant achievements are early milestones of personal power.[172]

Over the course of childhood, children learn and develop skills of self-management or personal control. This does not occur abruptly; children do not suddenly become autonomous.[173] Although the development of autonomy is thought to occur during adolescence,[174] the transfer of responsibility for self-management from parent to child is a slow process that begins much earlier.[175] For this reason, it is important that children share the control of some age-appropriate responsibilities. It is through this process that they become capable of controlling their lives.

Personal power also pertains to the way a child copes with stress and difficult situations. Some coping strategies are *problem-focused,* centering on problem-solving techniques such as information gathering. Other strategies are *emotion-*

	Infants and Toddlers (Birth to age 2)	Preschoolers (Ages 3 to 5)	Elementary-Age Children (Ages 6 to 11)
	FIGURE 27		
	Positive-Identity Assets through the Years		
37.	**Family has personal power**		**Personal power**
	Parent(s) feel they have control over things that happen to them and model coping skills, demonstrating healthy ways to deal with frustrations and challenges.		Child begins to feel he or she has control over "things that happen to me." Child begins to manage life's frustrations and challenges in ways that have positive results for the child and others.
38.	**Family models high self-esteem**		**Self-esteem**
	Parent(s) model high self-esteem and create an environment where the child can develop positive self-esteem, giving the child positive feedback and reinforcement about skills and competencies.		Child reports having a high self-esteem.
39.	**Family has a sense of purpose**		**Sense of purpose**
	Parent(s) report that their lives have purpose and model these beliefs through their behaviors.		Child reports that "my life has a purpose."
40.	**Family has a positive view of the future**		**Positive view of personal future**
	Parent(s) are optimistic about their personal future and work to provide a positive future for the child.		Child is optimistic about her or his personal future.

focused, involving talking about the problem, getting emotional support, or ruminating. Both types of strategies are important, depending on the type of problem at hand. Researchers have shown, however, that girls tend to employ more emotion-focused techniques, while boys use more problem-focused coping strategies.[176] Good coping strategies develop gradually over the course of childhood and are associated with psychological well-being in adolescence and adulthood.[177] Successful acquisition of these skills may be related to how many other assets the child may have.

One important aspect of personal power is "locus of control." This refers to *perceived* control— how people view the events around them. Attributing something that has happened to some factor that is within one's control is considered *internal* locus of control. For example, a child gets an "A" on a test and attributes that grade to her or his hard work and study, something the child has control of. Alternatively, attributing an event to something external, something a child has no control of, is considered *external* locus of control. In this case, the "A" on the test might be the result of luck or an accident.[178]

Much of the research pertaining to locus of control has focused on adults and adolescents. Researchers have suggested that the concept of locus of control may not fit entirely for children. Children do not necessarily make attributions on the basis of luck or chance. Instead, children are more concerned with or aware of who is in charge.[179]

An internalized sense of personal control is an important factor in identity development, sense of empowerment, and self-esteem. Extensive research links internal locus of control to a number of positive outcomes.[180] One study, for example, found that children who rely on or trust their own abilities or effort to influence events were more able to propose solutions to problems when in conflict with other children.[181]

▼ Asset No. 38: Self-esteem

Researcher Susan Harter has suggested that a positive sense of self is an essential component of healthy development during childhood and adolescence.[182] When children have opportunities to be involved in positive and supportive social relationships, develop life skills, be part of a group, and feel that they have something to contribute, their development of a sense of self-competence is enhanced.[183] Love, acceptance, support, and positive interactions all are building blocks for a child's self-esteem. "Self-esteem is shaped and reshaped as we interact with each other and our environment," write Nancy E. Curry and Carl N. Johnson. "Infants and toddlers are developing and consolidating an initial sense of self. Preschoolers are further expanding those images and school-age children are measuring themselves against new standards."[184]

Self-esteem involves the perceptions of one's abilities or strengths in a number of domains, such as physical attractiveness, academic competence, peer relationships, athletics, and behavior.[185] A child's self-esteem is affected by his or her feelings of self-competence in the domains he or she deems particularly important. For example, if playing softball is important to a young girl, and she does not feel that she is good at softball, her self-esteem will likely be affected.[186]

Positive messages to children about their skills and abilities are more likely to promote high self-esteem than are messages to children about their inadequacies.[187] In addition, beginning in the school-age years, children compare themselves with peers in terms of their competence at such things as academics or sports.[188] Having a sense of success at tasks and feeling competent also helps build self-efficacy, an important component of healthy self-esteem.

Researchers have observed gender differences in self-esteem, particularly in adolescence.[190] In her study of girls who attend the Emma Willard School in Troy, New York, Carol Gilligan observed that adolescence is a particularly crucial time in the development of self-esteem for girls. "Adolescence seems a watershed in female development, a time when girls are in danger of drowning or disappearing," Gilligan writes.[191]

Gilligan and her colleagues suggest that girls must be able to move beyond female stereotypes and balance their responsiveness to others with their responsiveness to their own needs. "Thus for girls to develop a clear sense of self in relationship with others means—at least within the mainstream of North American culture—to take on the problem of resistance and also to take up the question of what relationship means to themselves, to others, and to the world," Gilligan says.[192]

Although the bulk of Gilligan's work pertains to adolescent girls, her research suggests that adults should carefully consider how to nurture the self-esteem of all children from their birth. Children who have positive self-esteem during the early years are arguably less likely to suffer from declining self-esteem during adolescence. Nonetheless, the challenges of early adolescence may make some young people, particularly some girls, vulnerable to negative changes in self-esteem.[193]

> "Positive self-esteem comes from making the commitment to respect, accept, and love yourself completely. It is the best gift you can give yourself—and your children."[189]
>
> Louise Hart, Ph.D.
> Psychologist and self-esteem expert

▼ Asset No. 39: Sense of purpose
▼ Asset No. 40: Positive view of personal future

Children develop a sense of purpose through observation and internalization. If parents feel they have a sense of purpose, children tend to feel that their lives have meaning as well. In addition, parents who view their own futures positively and who aspire to make their children's lives full of opportunity and promise convey hope and optimism to their children.

Learning optimism is an essential part of identity formation. "When you teach your child optimism, you are teaching him to know himself, to be curious about his theory of himself and of the world," writes psychologist and researcher Martin E. P. Seligman. "You are teaching him to take an active stance in his world and to shape his own life, rather than be a passive recipient of what happens his way."[194]

Seligman developed a "pyramid of optimism" paradigm to show that a child develops a positive view of the future in a progressive, three-stage process that starts in infancy. The foundation for optimism is *mastery*, which gives a child a feeling of control over her or his environment. As soon as a child is old enough to articulate a "yes" or a "no," adults should give the child simple choices. Eating finger foods and, when the child is old enough, using eating utensils are early ways in which a child can feel a sense of mastery. Age-appropriate toys that require a child to manipulate something or cause something to happen (such as building blocks and crayons) also increase a sense of mastery. Appropriately challenging situations allow for the development of new skills.[195] In addition, helping children to work through difficult situations through play is another way to help them gain mastery over their environment. A visit to the doctor's office that requires a shot or blood test can be "mastered" by the child if she or he is allowed or encouraged to replay the experience through pretend play, such as pretending to give the parent or a stuffed animal or doll a shot.

The second tier of Seligman's optimism pyramid is *positivity*. Children who feel loved and accepted are more likely to feel good about themselves and about their futures. Seligman suggests that adults should love children unconditionally and praise them conditionally.[196] This means that praise should be contingent on the child's success and given in doses that fit the accomplishment. Seligman says adults should avoid finding something to praise when the child fails; instead, they should break the task into manageable steps and encourage the child to work toward success.

At the top of the optimism pyramid is *style*. Children who view the future and the world from a pessimistic point of view tend to see setbacks and failures as permanent, unchangeable, pervasive, and personal. They blame themselves for the difficulties that happen to them. Children who are optimistic, however, see setbacks as temporary and as changeable, affecting only a particular situation.[197] Unfounded or unreasonable optimism that prevents a child from recognizing a real problem can seriously hinder a child's development. Children should develop the ability to articulate problems, work to solve them, and at the same time to maintain a positive view of the future. Seligman's research has pointed to the importance of optimism in preventing depression later in life.

	FIGURE 29
	Ways to Promote Positive Identity

Age	Practical age-appropriate ideas
0–1	• Love, respect, and accept children unconditionally.
	• Delight in each child's unique personality.
	• Create positive interactions. Play together in ways that make young children laugh and enjoy the time together.
1–2	• Focus on the behavior, do not blame the child, when changing children's inappropriate behavior.
	• Dwell on what children do right instead of what they do wrong.
	• Create an atmosphere that is loving, supportive, and affirming so that children enjoy and feel good about their environment.
3–5	• Encourage children to begin to take pride in their cultural heritage.
	• Break new tasks and skills into small, manageable steps that children can master without becoming too frustrated.
	• Ask children how they feel about the events in their lives. Encourage them to identify more positive examples than negative ones.
6–11	• Encourage children to identify inspirational, positive role models to emulate.
	• Ask children how they feel about their future. Encourage them to take concrete steps to make their future something positive to look forward to.
	• Encourage children to seek out answers and solutions when they face obstacles or difficult times.

Starting Out Right: Developmental Assets for Children

Moving Forward

Chapter 11 focuses on how assets may be in short supply for many children and how we can mobilize our nation to build assets.

A Future of Hope for Children

tarting Out Right has been developed to advance the dialogue about how our society can better care for its children. In bringing together the collective wisdom of many people and fields, this report presents a new paradigm for examining the place of children in the United States and identifying where the nation needs to invest time, creativity, and resources to ensure that all children have a positive foundation for life.

The developmental asset framework for children would need to be rigorously tested, refined, and validated for us to have the same confidence that we have in the framework for adolescents. While Search Institute has documented the importance of developmental assets in adolescents, it has not done so in children. Without empirical data, we do not know how well families and communities are providing assets for children. Nevertheless, our extensive research on adolescents, our review of other research, and the views of experts and practitioners all suggest that developmental assets may be in short supply for many American children. This suggests that all of us who care about young people and the future of our nation need to mobilize our society to provide these assets for every child in every community.

▼ Next Steps

We can only speculate on all the possible uses for the children's assets framework, but we propose three areas in which next steps are appropriate:

1. The assets paradigm offers people and organizations committed to children a chance to advance a new dialogue about the way our nation addresses children's issues. We believe this dialogue should explore questions such as:

    • What would happen if the U.S. Congress and the president used these assets as filters for making policy and budgetary decisions that affect children and families?

What Children and Families Need

"Strong families and communities are essential to the healthy development of our youngest children," says the Carnegie Task Force on Meeting the Needs of Young Children. The task force recommends four key areas that constitute essential starting points for children and families:

◆ Promote responsible parenthood;

◆ Guarantee quality child care choices;

◆ Ensure good health and protection; and

◆ Mobilize communities to support young children and their families.

Information from Carnegie Task Force on Meeting the Needs of Young Children, *Starting Points: Meeting the Needs of Our Youngest Children* (Waldorf, Md.: Carnegie Corporation of New York, 1994), 105.

- How might communities come together to create a shared vision of ensuring that all children and youth within the community have a strong asset foundation?

- How would schools, child care centers, religious congregations, and other programs and services for children change if these assets were integrated into planning, training, implementation, and evaluation activities?

- How might parents be supported and educated to be effective asset builders for their children? How might parents spend their time and energy differently if they knew the importance of building these assets in their children? How might our corporations and industries help provide the supports so that their employees who are parents can nurture their children?

- How might neighbors and friends interact differently with children if concerted energy were directed toward educating the public about everyone's power to build assets in children?

2. Although the asset framework for children is an exploratory conceptualization and although it is not an exhaustive list of everything children need, it still is likely to be a useful tool for educating parents, child care workers, educators, and others who work with children. This education needs to focus on helping adults internalize a vision for healthy children, equipping them with the skills they need to build these assets, and motivating them with the message that the caring, support, and guidance that they offer to children are critically important.

3. Dozens of communities across the United States have begun asset-building initiatives based on Search Institute's framework of assets for adolescents with support from Search Institute's *Healthy Communities • Healthy Youth* initiative. Most of these initiatives are committed to building assets not only in adolescents, but also in younger children. This new framework offers these initiatives a beginning tool for helping these efforts to be developmentally responsive to younger ages. We encourage the leaders of these initiatives to explore how the children's assets can best be integrated into their efforts; we also encourage feedback and dialogue about how this "lens" works.

▼ Creating Stronger Communities

Strong families and strong communities are essential for raising healthy children and helping them to maneuver through the maze of changes and challenges they encounter during childhood and adolescence. The developmental assets framework is intended to help parents, other adults, and communities create

> *"It is long past time for us to join together as an entire nation and in every community to establish an ethic of service and achievement and to help support strong families for all our children."* [198]
>
> *Marian Wright Edelman*
> *Founder and president,*
> *Children's Defense Fund*

better environments, supports, and programs to ensure that all children have the foundation they need to start out right in life.

Although parents and caregivers are the major influence on young children, everyone in the community can help provide parents and caregivers essential support, training, and information. Schools, child care providers, religious congregations, community programs, and families can work together to ensure that each child has access to the skills, competencies, relationships, and values needed to become a competent, caring, and responsible adult. The well-being of our communities and the future of our society depend on it.

Charts

Developmental Assets for Infants and Toddlers (Birth to Age 2)

Asset Type	Asset Name and Definition

E X T E R N A L   A S S E T S

Support

1.	**Family support**—Family life provides high levels of love and support.
2.	**Positive family communication**—Parent(s) communicate with the child in positive ways. Parent(s) respond immediately to the child and respect the child.
3.	**Other adult resources**—Parent(s) receive support from three or more nonparent adults and ask for help when needed. The child receives love and comfort from at least one nonparent adult.
4.	**Caring neighborhood**—Child experiences caring neighbors.
5.	**Caring out-of-home climate**—Child is in caring, encouraging environments outside the home.
6.	**Parent involvement in out-of-home situations**—Parent(s) are actively involved in helping the child succeed in situations outside the home.

Empowerment

7.	**Children valued**—The family places the child at the center of family life.
8.	**Child has role in family life**—The family involves the child in family life.
9.	**Service to others**—Parent(s) serve others in the community.
10.	**Safety**—Child has a safe environment at home, in out-of-home settings, and in the neighborhood.

Boundaries and Expectations

11.	**Family boundaries**—Parent(s) are aware of the child's preferences and adapt the environment to best suit the child's needs. Parent(s) begin setting limits as the child becomes mobile.
12.	**Out-of-home boundaries**—Child care and other out-of-home environments have clear rules and consequences while consistently providing the child with appropriate stimulation and enough rest.
13.	**Neighborhood boundaries**—Neighbors take responsibility for monitoring child's behavior as the child begins to play and interact outside the home.
14.	**Adult role models**—Parent(s) and other adults model positive, responsible behavior.
15.	**Positive peer observation**—Child observes positive peer interactions of siblings and other children and has opportunities for beginning interactions with children of various ages.
16.	**Expectations for growth**—Parent(s) are realistic in their expectations of development at this age. Parent(s) encourage development but do not push the child beyond his or her own pace.

Constructive Use of Time

17.	**Creative activities**—Parent(s) daily expose the child to music, art, or other creative activities.
18.	**Out-of-home activities**—Parent(s) expose the child to limited but stimulating situations outside of the home. Family attends events with the child's needs in mind.
19.	**Religious community**—Family attends religious programs or services on a regular basis while keeping the child's needs in mind.
20.	**Positive, supervised time at home**—Parent(s) supervise the child at all times and provide predictable and enjoyable routines at home

Continued

Developmental Assets for Infants and Toddlers, Continued

Asset Type	Asset Name and Definition

I N T E R N A L A S S E T S

Commitment to Learning

21.	**Achievement expectation**—Family members are motivated to do well at work, school, and in the community, and model this to the child.
22.	**Engagement expectation**—The family models responsive and attentive attitudes at work, school, in the community, and at home.
23.	**Stimulating activity**—Parent(s) encourage the child to explore and provide stimulating toys that match the child's emerging skills. Parent(s) are sensitive to the child's level of development and tolerance for movement, sounds, and duration of activity.
24.	**Enjoyment of learning**—Parent(s) enjoy learning, and demonstrate this through their own learning activities.
25.	**Reading for pleasure**—Parent(s) read to the child daily in enjoyable ways.

Positive Values

26.	**Family values caring**—Parent(s) convey their beliefs about helping others by modeling their helping behaviors.
27.	**Family values equality and social justice**—Parent(s) place a high value on promoting equality and reducing hunger and poverty, and model these beliefs.
28.	**Family values integrity**—Parent(s) act on convictions and stand up for their beliefs, and communicate and model this in the family.
29.	**Family values honesty**—Parent(s) tell the truth and convey their belief in honesty through their actions.
30.	**Family values responsibility**—Parent(s) accept and take personal responsibility.
31.	**Family values healthy lifestyle and sexual attitudes**—Parent(s) love the child, setting the foundation for the child to develop healthy sexual attitudes and beliefs. Parent(s) model, monitor, and teach the importance of good health habits, such as providing good nutritional choices and adequate rest and play time.

Social Competencies

32.	**Planning and decision-making observation**—Parent(s) make all safety and care decisions for the child and then model these behaviors. Parent(s) allow the child to make simple choices as the child becomes more independently mobile.
33.	**Interpersonal observation**—Parent(s) model positive and constructive interactions with other people. Parent(s) accept and are responsive to the child's expression of feelings, interpreting those expressions as cues to the child's needs.
34.	**Cultural observation**—Parent(s) have knowledge of and are comfortable with people of different cultural/racial/ethnic backgrounds, and model this to the child.
35.	**Resistance observation**—Parent(s) model resistance skills by their own behaviors. Parent(s) are not overwhelmed by the child's needs and thereby demonstrate appropriate resistance skills.
36.	**Peaceful conflict resolution observation**—Parent(s) behave in acceptable, nonviolent ways and assist the child to develop these skills when faced with challenging or frustrating circumstances by helping child solve problems.

Positive Identity

37.	**Family has personal power**—Parent(s) feel they have control over things that happen to them and model coping skills, demonstrating healthy ways to deal with frustrations and challenges.
38.	**Family models high self-esteem**—Parent(s) model high self-esteem and create an environment where the child can develop positive self-esteem, giving the child positive feedback and reinforcement about skills and competencies.
39.	**Family has a sense of purpose**—Parent(s) report that their lives have purpose and model these beliefs through their behaviors.
40.	**Family has a positive view of the future**—Parent(s) are optimistic about their personal future and work to provide a positive future for the child.

Developmental Assets for Preschoolers (Ages 3 to 5)

Asset Type	Asset Name and Definition

E X T E R N A L A S S E T S

Support

1.	**Family support**—Family life provides high levels of love and support.
2.	**Positive family communication**—Parent(s) and child communicate positively. Child seeks out parent(s) for assistance with difficult tasks or situations.
3.	**Other adult resources**—Child receives support from at least one nonparent adult. Parent(s) have support from individuals outside the home.
4.	**Caring neighborhood**—Child experiences caring neighbors.
5.	**Caring out-of-home climate**—Child is in caring, encouraging environments outside the home.
6.	**Parent involvement in out-of-home situations**—Parent(s) are actively involved in helping child succeed in situations outside the home.

Empowerment

7.	**Children valued**—Parent(s) and other adults value and appreciate children.
8.	**Children given useful roles** —Parent(s) and other adults take child into account when making decisions and gradually include the child in decisions.
9.	**Service to others**—The family serves others in the community together.
10.	**Safety**—Child has a safe environment at home, in out-of-home settings, and in the neighborhood.

Boundaries and Expectations

11.	**Family boundaries**—Family has clear rules and consequences. Family monitors the child and consistently demonstrates appropriate behavior through modeling and limit setting.
12.	**Out-of-home boundaries**—Neighbors, child care, preschool, and community provide clear rules and consequences.
13.	**Neighborhood boundaries**—Neighbors take responsibility for monitoring the child's behavior.
14.	**Adult role models**—Parent(s) and other adults model positive, responsible behavior.
15.	**Positive peer interactions**—Child's interactions with other children are encouraged and promoted. Child is given opportunities to play with other children in a safe, well-supervised setting.
16.	**Expectations for growth**—Adults have realistic expectations of development at this age. Parent(s), caregivers, and other adults encourage child to achieve and develop his or her unique talents.

Constructive Use of Time

17.	**Creative activities**—Child participates in music, art, or dramatic play on a daily basis.
18.	**Out-of-home activities**—Child interacts with children outside the family. Family attends events with the child's needs in mind.
19.	**Religious community**—Family attends religious programs or services on a regular basis while keeping the child's needs in mind.
20.	**Positive, supervised time at home**—Child is supervised by an adult at all times. Child spends most evenings and weekends at home with parent(s) in predictable, fun, enjoyable routines.

Continued

Starting Out Right: Developmental Assets for Children

Developmental Assets for Preschoolers, Continued

Asset Type	Asset Name and Definition

INTERNAL ASSETS

Commitment to Learning

21. **Achievement expectation**—Parent(s) and other adults convey and reinforce expectations to do well at work, school, in the community, and within the family.

22. **Engagement expectation**—The family models responsive and attentive attitudes at work, school, in the community, and at home.

23. **Stimulating activity**—Parent(s) and other adults encourage the child to explore and provide stimulating toys that match the child's emerging skills. Parent(s) and other adults are sensitive to the child's level of development.

24. **Enjoyment of learning**—Parent(s) and other adults enjoy learning and engage the child in learning activities.

25. **Reading for pleasure**—Caring adult(s) read to the child for at least 30 minutes a day.

Positive Values

26. **Family values caring**—Child is encouraged to express sympathy for someone who is distressed and to share his or her possessions with others.

27. **Family values equality and social justice**—Parent(s) place a high value on promoting equality and reducing hunger and poverty, and model these beliefs.

28. **Family values integrity**—Parent(s) act on convictions and stand up for their beliefs, and communicate and model this in the family.

29. **Family values honesty**—Child learns the difference between truth and lying.

30. **Family values responsibility**—Child learns that actions have an effect on other people.

31. **Family values healthy lifestyle and sexual attitudes**—Parent(s) and other adults model, monitor, and teach the importance of good health habits. Child learns healthy sexual attitudes and beliefs and to respect others.

Social Competencies

32. **Planning and decision-making practice**—Child begins to make simple choices, solve simple problems, and develop simple plans at an age-appropriate level.

33. **Interpersonal interactions**—Child plays and interacts with other children and adults. Child freely expresses feelings and is taught to articulate feelings verbally. Parent(s) and other adults model and teach empathy.

34. **Cultural interactions**—Child is positively exposed to information and people of different cultural/racial/ethnic backgrounds.

35. **Resistance practice**—Child is taught to resist participating in behavior that is inappropriate or dangerous.

36. **Peaceful conflict resolution practice**—Parent(s) and other adults model peaceful conflict resolution. Child is taught and begins to practice nonviolent, acceptable ways to deal with challenging and frustrating situations.

Positive Identity

37. **Family has personal power**—Parent(s) feel they have control over things that happen to them and model coping skills, demonstrating healthy ways to deal with frustrations and challenges.

38. **Family models high self-esteem**—Parent(s) model high self-esteem and create an environment where the child can develop positive self-esteem, giving the child positive feedback and reinforcement about skills and competencies.

39. **Family has a sense of purpose**—Parent(s) report that their lives have purpose and model these beliefs through their behaviors.

40. **Family has a positive view of the future**—Parent(s) are optimistic about their personal future and work to provide a positive future for the child.

Developmental Assets for Elementary-Age Children (Ages 6 to 11)

Asset Type	Asset Name and Definition

E X T E R N A L   A S S E T S

Support

1. **Family support**—Family life provides high levels of love and support.
2. **Positive family communication**—Parent(s) and child communicate positively. Child is willing to seek parent(s) advice and counsel.
3. **Other adult relationships**—Child receives support from nonparent adults.
4. **Caring neighborhood**—Child experiences caring neighbors.
5. **Caring school climate**—School provides a caring, encouraging environment.
6. **Parent involvement in schooling**—Parent(s) are actively involved in helping child succeed in school.

Empowerment

7. **Community values children**—Child feels that the community values and appreciates children.
8. **Children given useful roles**—Child is included in family decisions and is given useful roles at home and in the community.
9. **Service to others**—Child and parent(s) serve others and the community.
10. **Safety**—Child is safe at home, at school, and in the neighborhood.

Boundaries and Expectations

11. **Family boundaries**—Family has clear rules and consequences, and monitors the child's whereabouts.
12. **School boundaries**—School provides clear rules and consequences.
13. **Neighborhood boundaries**—Neighbors take responsibility for monitoring the child's behavior.
14. **Adult role models**—Parent(s) and other adults model positive, responsible behavior.
15. **Positive peer interactions**—Child plays with children who model responsible behavior.
16. **Expectations for growth**—Adults have realistic expectations of development at this age. Parent(s), caregivers, and other adults encourage child to achieve and develop his or her unique talents.

Constructive Use of Time

17. **Creative activities**—Child participates in music, arts, or drama three or more hours each week through home and out-of-home activities.
18. **Child programs**—Child spends one hour or more per week in extracurricular school activities or structured community programs.
19. **Religious community**—Family attends religious programs or services for at least one hour per week.
20. **Positive, supervised time at home**—Child spends most evenings and weekends at home with parent(s) in predictable and enjoyable routines.

Continued

Developmental Assets for Elementary-Age Children, Continued

Asset Type	Asset Name and Definition

I N T E R N A L   A S S E T S

Commitment to Learning

21.	**Achievement motivation**—Child is motivated to do well in school.
22.	**School engagement**—Child is responsive, attentive, and actively engaged in learning.
23.	**Homework**—Child does homework when it is assigned.
24.	**Bonding to school**—Child cares about her or his school.
25.	**Reading for pleasure**—Child and a caring adult read together for at least 30 minutes a day. Child also enjoys reading without an adult's involvement.

Positive Values

26.	**Caring**—Child is encouraged to help other people and to share her or his possessions.
27.	**Equality and social justice**—Child begins to show interest in making the community a better place.
28.	**Integrity**—Child begins to act on convictions and stand up for her or his beliefs.
29.	**Honesty**—Child begins to value honesty and act accordingly.
30.	**Responsibility**—Child begins to accept and take personal responsibility for age-appropriate tasks.
31.	**Healthy lifestyle and sexual attitudes**—Child begins to value good health habits. Child learns healthy sexual attitudes and beliefs and to respect others.

Social Competencies

32.	**Planning and decision-making**—Child learns beginning skills of how to plan ahead and makes decisions at an appropriate developmental level.
33.	**Interpersonal competence**—Child interacts with adults and children and can make friends. Child expresses and articulates feelings in appropriate ways and empathizes with others.
34.	**Cultural competence**—Child has knowledge of and comfort with people of different cultural/racial/ethnic backgrounds.
35.	**Resistance skills**—Child begins to develop the ability to resist negative peer pressure and dangerous situations.
36.	**Peaceful conflict resolution**—Child attempts to resolve conflict nonviolently.

Positive Identity

37.	**Personal power**—Child begins to feel he or she has control over "things that happen to me." Child begins to manage life's frustrations and challenges in ways that have positive results for the child and others.
38.	**Self-esteem**—Child reports having a high self-esteem.
39.	**Sense of purpose**—Child reports that "my life has a purpose."
40.	**Positive view of personal future**—Child is optimistic about her or his personal future.

Developmental Assets for Adolescents (Ages 12–18)

Asset Type	Asset Name and Definition

E X T E R N A L   A S S E T S

Support

1. **Family support**—Family life provides high levels of love and support.
2. **Positive family communication**—Young person and her or his parent(s) communicate positively, and young person is willing to seek advice and counsel from parent(s).
3. **Other adult relationships**—Young person receives support from three or more nonparent adults.
4. **Caring neighborhood**—Young person experiences caring neighbors.
5. **Caring school climate**—School provides a caring, encouraging environment.
6. **Parent involvement in schooling**—Parent(s) are actively involved in helping young person succeed in school.

Empowerment

7. **Community values youth**—Young person perceives that adults in the community value youth.
8. **Youth as resources**—Young people are given useful roles in the community.
9. **Service to others**—Young person serves in the community one hour or more per week.
10. **Safety**—Young person feels safe at home, school, and in the neighborhood.

Boundaries and Expectations

11. **Family boundaries**—Family has clear rules and consequences, and monitors young people's whereabouts.
12. **School boundaries**—School provides clear rules and consequences.
13. **Neighborhood boundaries**—Neighbors take responsibility for monitoring young people's behavior.
14. **Adult role models**—Parent(s) and other adults model positive, responsible behavior.
15. **Positive peer influence**—Young person's best friends model responsible behavior.
16. **High expectations**—Both parent(s) and teachers encourage the young person to do well.

Constructive Use of Time

17. **Creative activities**—Young person spends three or more hours per week in lessons or practice in music, theater, or other arts.
18. **Youth programs**—Young person spends three hours or more hours per week in sports, clubs, or organizations at school and/or in community organizations.
19. **Religious community**—Young person spends one or more hours per week in activities in a religious institution.
20. **Time at home**—Young person is out with friends "with nothing special to do," two or fewer nights per week.

Continued

Developmental Assets for Adolescents, Continued

Asset Type	Asset Name and Definition

I N T E R N A L   A S S E T S

Commitment to Learning

21.	**Achievement motivation**—Young person is motivated to do well in school.
22.	**School engagement**—Young person is actively engaged in learning.
23.	**Homework**—Young person reports doing at least one hour of homework every school day.
24.	**Bonding to school**—Young person cares about her or his school.
25.	**Reading for pleasure**—Young person reads for pleasure three or more hours per week.

Positive Values

26.	**Caring**—Young person places high value on helping other people.
27.	**Equality and social justice**—Young person places high value on promoting equality and reducing hunger and poverty.
28.	**Integrity**—Young person acts on convictions and stands up for her or his beliefs.
29.	**Honesty**—Young person "tells the truth even when it is not easy."
30.	**Responsibility**—Young person accepts and takes personal responsibility.
31.	**Restraint**—Young person believes it is important not to be sexually active or to use alcohol or other drugs.

Social Competencies

32.	**Planning and decision-making**—Young person knows how to plan ahead and make choices.
33.	**Interpersonal competence**—Young person has empathy, sensitivity, and friendship skills.
34.	**Cultural competence**—Young person has knowledge of and comfort with people of different cultural/racial/ethnic backgrounds.
35.	**Resistance skills**—Young person can resist negative peer pressure and dangerous situations.
36.	**Peaceful conflict resolution**—Young person seeks to resolve conflict non-violently.

Positive Identity

37.	**Personal power**—Young person feels he or she has control over "things that happen to me."
38.	**Self-esteem**—Young person reports having a high self-esteem.
39.	**Sense of purpose**—Young person reports "my life has a purpose."
40.	**Positive view of personal future**—Young person is optimistic about her or his personal future.

References and Resources

The pages that follow include notes for each chapter, recommended reading, and a list of asset-building resources.

Notes

Chapter 1

1. David Elkind, *The Hurried Child* (Reading, Mass.: Addison-Wesley, 1981), 200.

2. Carnegie Task Force on Meeting the Needs of Young Children, *Starting Points: Meeting the Needs of Our Youngest Children* (Waldorf, Md.: Carnegie Corporation of New York, 1994), 3.

3. J. P. Chonkoff., "The Biological Substrate and Physical Health in Middle Childhood," *Development During Middle Childhood: The Years from Six to Twelve*, ed. W. Andrew Collins (Washington, D.C.: National Academy of Sciences Press, 1984), 24–69; Raymond P. Lorion and William Saltman, "Children's Exposure to Community Violence: Following a Path from Concern to Research to Action," *Psychiatry* 56 (1993): 55–65; Janet K. Wiig and Kristi Lahti-Johnson, *Delinquent Under 10 in Hennepin County: A Statistical Analysis and Practices and Experiences of Police Jurisdictions* (Minneapolis: Office of the Hennepin County Attorney, 1995).

4. Marian Wright Edelman, *Guide My Feet: Prayers and Meditations on Loving and Working for Children* (Boston: Beacon, 1995).

5. Peter L. Benson, *The Troubled Journey: A Portrait of 6th–12th Grade Youth* (Minneapolis: Search Institute, 1990, 1993).

6. Peter L. Benson, *Uniting Communities for Youth* (Minneapolis: Search Institute, 1995), 4.

7. Peter L. Benson, *Developmental Assets among Minneapolis Youth: The Urgency of Promoting Healthy Community* (Minneapolis: Search Institute, 1996); Peter L. Benson, *Developmental Assets among Albuquerque Youth: The Urgency of Promoting Healthy Community* (Minneapolis: Search Institute, 1996). Communities and school districts can assess the assets of their students using Search Institute's survey *Profiles of Student Life: Attitudes and Behaviors,* which has been the basis for the research on developmental assets for adolescents, and which now uses the expanded, 40-asset, framework. For information, contact Search Institute at 800-888-7828 (or send e-mail to search@search-institute.org).

8. This committee in St. Louis Park, Minn., included Karen Atkinson, coordinator of Children First; Joan Finch, third-grade teacher; Harriet Griffin, kindergarten teacher; Ruth Hansen, elementary program specialist; Frank Johnson, principal at Peter Hobart Primary Center; Jackie Johnston, family services manager for community education; Jolene Roehlkepartain, parent educator and coauthor of this report; Jodi Schaefer, learning readiness educator; and Anne Stokes, Ph.D., of the community's early childhood and family education program. The committee was convened in cooperation with Children First, the city's asset-building initiative. St. Louis Park was the first community in the nation to adopt Search Institute's developmental assets as a framework for community action.

9. The following experts gave extensive feedback on earlier drafts of this framework: Louise Bates Ames, Ph.D., cofounder of the Gesell Institute of Human Development in New Haven, Conn.; W. Andrew Collins, Ph.D., professor of child psychology at the Institute of Child Development, University of Minnesota; Martha Farrell Erickson, Ph.D., director of the Children, Youth, and Family Consortium, University of Minnesota; Daniel Repinski, Ph.D., assistant professor of psychology, State University of New York, Geneseo; Mary Sheedy Kurcinka, parent educator, author, and the former director of Minnesota's Early Childhood Family Education programs; Jean Illsley Clarke, parent educator and the author of many parenting books; Connie Dawson, Ph.D., specialist in infant attachment; Brenda Holben, prevention coordinator for the Cherry Creek School District in Englewood, Colo.; and Judy Carter, former executive director of the Family Resource Coalition, Chicago.

10. For a comprehensive presentation of this effort, see Peter L. Benson, *Creating Healthy Communities for Children and Adolescents* (San Francisco: Jossey-Bass, forthcoming 1997).

11. The 40-asset framework was first tested and reported on in studies of youth in two major cities. See Benson, *Developmental Assets among Minneapolis Youth;* and Benson, *Developmental Assets among Albuquerque Youth.* Search Institute resources will be revised beginning in 1997 to reflect this expanded framework.

12. David A. Hamburg, *A Developmental Strategy to Prevent Lifelong Damage* (New York: Carnegie Corporation of New York, 1995), 7.

13. Comments may be sent to Nancy Leffert, *Starting Out Right,* Search Institute, 700 S. Third Street, Suite 210, Minneapolis, MN 55415-1138 (e-mail to nleffert@search-institute.org, or by fax to 612-376-8956). Readers may wish to use the form on page 115.

Chapter 2

14. Benson, *Developmental Assets among Minneapolis Youth;* Benson, *Developmental Assets among Albuquerque Youth.*

15. W. Andrew Collins, Michael L. Harris, and Amy Susman, "Parenting During Middle Childhood," in *Handbook of Parenting*, vol. 1, ed. Marc Bornstein (Mahwah, N.J.: Lawrence Erlbaum, 1995), 66.

16. Daniel Goleman, *Emotional Intelligence* (New York: Bantam, 1995), 256.

17. Robert Plomin, *Nature and Nurture: An Introduction to Human Behavioral Genetics* (Pacific Grove, Calif.: Brooks/Cole, 1990).

18. Ludwig Von Bertalanffy, *General Systems Theory* (New York: Braziller, 1968).

19. Emmy E. Werner and Ruth S. Smith, *Vulnerable but Invincible: A Longitudinal Study of Resilient Children and Youth* (New York: Adams Bannister Cox, 1982).

20. John Bowlby, *Attachment and Loss,* vol. 3 (New York: Basic, 1980); Michael Rutter, "Continuities and Discontinuities in Socio-Emotional Development: Empirical and Conceptual Perspectives," in *Continuities and Discontinuities in Development,* ed. Robert N. Emde and Robert J. Harmon (New York: Plenum, 1983); L. Alan Sroufe and Michael Rutter, "The Domain of Developmental Psychopathology," *Child Development* 55 (1984): 17–29.

21. Benson, *Developmental Assets among Albuquerque Youth*, 23.

22. Ibid.

23. Annie E. Casey Foundation, *Kids Count Data Book: State Profiles of Well-Being* (Baltimore: Annie E. Casey Foundation, 1996).

24. Werner and Smith, *Vulnerable but Invincible.*

25. Michael Rutter and Henri Giller, *Juvenile Delinquency: Trends and Perspectives* (New York: Guilford, 1983).

26. Ann S. Masten, Karen M. Best, and Norman Garmezy, "Resilience and Development: Contributions from the Study of Children Who Overcome Adversity," in *Development & Psychopathology* 2, no. 4 (1990): 425–44.

27. Bowlby, *Attachment and Loss*; Rutter, "Continuities and Discontinuities"; Sroufe and Rutter, "The Domain of Developmental Psychopathology."

28. This material is adapted from Dale A. Blyth and Eugene C. Roehlkepartain, *Healthy Communities • Healthy Youth* (Minneapolis: Search Institute, 1996).

Chapter 3

29. Mary D. S. Ainsworth, Mary D. Blehar, Everett Waters, and S. Wall, *Patterns of Attachment: A Psychological Study of the Strange Situation* (Hillsdale, N.J.: Lawrence Erlbaum, 1978); Bowlby, *Attachment and Loss;* Margaret S. Mahler, Fred Pine, and Anni Bergman, *The Psychological Birth of the Human Infant: Symbiosis and Individuation* (New York: Basic, 1975); René A. Spitz, *The First Year of Life: A Psychoanalytic Study of Normal and Deviant Development of Object Relations* (New York: International Universities Press, 1965); L. Alan Sroufe and June Fleeson, "Attachment and the Construction of Relationships," in *Relationships and Development*, ed. Willard Hartup and Zick Rubin (New York: Cambridge University Press, 1986), 51–71.

30. Urie Bronfenbrenner, "Beyond the Deficit Model in Child and Family Policy," *Teachers College Record* 81, no. 1 (1979): 95–104.

31. Joseph Goldstein, Anna Freud, and Albert Solnit, *Beyond the Best Interests of the Child* (New York: Free Press, 1973), 12.

32. Anna Freud, *Infants Without Families: Reports on the Hampstead Nurseries (1939–1945)* (New York: International Universities Press, 1973).

33. Spitz, *The First Year of Life.* See also Mahler, Pine, and Bergman, *Psychological Birth of the Human Infant.*

34. Freud, *Infants Without Families,* 38.

35. Mary D. S. Ainsworth, "The Effects of Maternal Deprivation: A Review of Findings and Controversy in the Context of Research Strategy," in W.H.O. Public Health Papers, no. 14, *Deprivation of Maternal Care: A Reassessment of Its Effects* (Geneva: World Health Organization, 1962); Selma H. Fraiberg, *Every Child's Birthright: In Defense of Mothering* (New York: Basic, 1977).

36. Silvia M. Bell and Mary D. S. Ainsworth, "Infant Crying and Maternal Responsiveness," in *Child Development and Behavior*, 2d ed., ed. Freda Rebelsky and Lynn Dormon (New York: Knopf, 1973); idem, "Infant Crying and Maternal Responsiveness," in *Child Development* 43, no. 4 (1972): 1171–90.

37. Carole J. Litt, "Theories of Transitional Object Attachment: An Overview," *International Journal of Behavioral Development* 9, no. 3 (1986): 383–99; Donald W. Winnicott, "Transitional Objects and Transitional Phenomena: A Study of the First Not-Me Possession," *International Journal of Psychoanalysis* 34 (1953): 89–97.

38. Ibid.; Spitz, *First Year of Life.*

39. Alison Clarke-Stewart, *Daycare*, rev. ed. (Cambridge, Mass.: Harvard University Press, 1993); Carollee Howes, "Relations Between Early Child Care and Schooling," *Developmental Psychology* 24 (1988): 53–57; Deborah Phillips, Kathleen McCartney, and Sandra Scarr, "Child-Care Quality and Children's Social Development," *Developmental Psychology* 23 (1987): 537–43.

40. Diana Baumrind, "Current Patterns of Parental Authority," *Developmental Psychology Monographs* 4, nos. 1, 2 (1971).

41. Sanford Dornbusch, Philip Ritter, P. Herbert Liederman, Donald F. Roberts, and Michael J. Fraleigh, "The Relation of Parenting Style to Adolescent School Performance," *Child Development* 58 (1987), 1244–57; Laurence Steinberg, Julie D. Elmen, and Nina S. Mounts, "Authoritative Parenting, Psychosocial Maturity, and Academic Success among Adolescents," *Child Development* 60 (1989): 1424–36.

42. Tiffany M. Field, "Touch Therapies across the Life Span," in *Handbook of Diversity Issues in Health Psychology*, ed. Pamela M. Kato and Traci Mann (New York: Plenum, 1996), 49–67.

43. Tiffany M. Field, Saul M. Schanberg, Frank Scafidi, et al., "Tactile/Kinesthetic Stimulation Effects on Preterm Neonates," *Pediatrics* 77, no. 5 (December 1984): 654–58.

44. Henri J. M. Nouwen, *Reaching Out* (Garden City, N.Y.: Doubleday, 1975), 56.

45. Erika Hoff-Ginsburg, "Function and Structure in Maternal Speech: Their Relation to the Child's Development of Syntax," *Developmental Psychology* 22 (1986): 155–63.

46. Leah Matas, Richard A. Arend, and L. Alan Sroufe, "Continuity of Adaptation in the Second Year: The Relationship Between Quality of Attachment and Later Competence," *Child Development* 49 (1978): 547–56.

47. Collins, Harris, and Susman, "Parenting During Middle Childhood," 67.

48. Robin Westen, "Laughing Matters," *Sesame Street Parents' Guide,* no. 227 (September 1993): 44.

49. Bronfenbrenner, "Beyond the Deficit Model."

50. Margaret K. McKim, "Transition to What? New Parents' Problems in the First Year," *Family Relations* 36 (1987): 23–24.

51. Ibid., 25.

52. J. J. Galbo, "Adolescents' Perceptions of Significant Adults: A Review of the Literature," *Adolescence* 19 (1984): 951–70.

53. Peter C. Scales and Judith L. Gibbons, "Extended Family Members and Unrelated Adults in the Lives of Young Adolescents: A Research Agenda," *Journal of Early Adolescence* 16, no. 4 (1996): 365–89.

54. Ibid.

55. Peter L. Benson, David J. Mangen, and Dorothy L. Williams, *Adults Who Influence Youth: Perspectives from 5th–12th-Grade Students* (Minneapolis: Search Institute, 1986).

56. Joyce L. Epstein, "Parent Involvement: What Research Says to Administrators," *Education and Urban Society* 19 (1987): 119–36.

57. Richard Koestner, Carol Franz, and Joel Weinberger, "The Family Origins of Empathic Concern: A 26-Year Longitudinal Study," *Journal of Personality and Social Psychology* 58, no. 4 (1990): 709–17.

58. Joyce L. Epstein, "What Principals Should Know about Parent Involvement," *Principal* 66 (1987): 6–9.

59. David L. Stevenson and David P. Baker, "The Family-School Relation and the Child's School Performance," Special Issue: Schools and Development, *Child Development* 58, no. 5 (1987): 1348–57.

Chapter 4

60. Charlotte R. Wallinga and Anne L. Sweaney, "A Sense of Real Accomplishment: Young Children as Productive Family Members," *Young Children* 41, no. 1 (1985): 3–8.

61. Lee Salk, *Familyhood* (New York: Simon & Schuster, 1992), 39.

62. Wallinga and Sweaney,"A Sense of Real Accomplishment."

63. Ibid.

64. Susan J. Ellis, Anne Weisbord, and Katherine H. Noyes, *Children as Volunteers: Preparing for Community Service,* rev. ed. (Philadelphia: Energize, 1991), 1.

65. *Volunteering Family Style* (Washington, D.C.: Points of Light Foundation, n.d.).

66. Burton L. White, *The New First Three Years of Life* (New York: Fireside, 1995), 340.

67. Ellis, Weisbord, and Noyes, *Children as Volunteers*, 17–22.

68. Ibid., 59–60.

69. Anna C. Fick and Sarah M. Thomas, "Growing Up in a Violent Environment: Relationship to Health-Related Beliefs and Behaviors," *Youth & Society* 27, no. 2 (1995), 136–47.

70. Nina Darnton, "The End of Innocence," *Newsweek Special Issue* 117, no. 26 (Summer 1991): 62.

71. Elkind, *The Hurried Child.*

72. Ibid.

Chapter 5

73. White, *The New First Three Years of Life,* 268.

74. Ibid.

75. Leon Kuczynski and Grazyna Kochanska, "Development of Children's Non-Compliance Strategies from Toddlerhood to Age 5," *Developmental Psychology* 26 (1990): 398–408.

76. White, *The New First Three Years of Life,* 14.

77. Celia A. Brownell and Ernestine Brown, "Peers and Play in Infants and Toddlers," in *Handbook of Social Development: A Lifespan Perspective*, ed. Vincent B. Van Hasselt and Michel Hersen (New York: Plenum, 1992), 183–200.

78. Ibid.

79. Marian Radke-Yarrow, Carolyn Zahn-Waxler, and Michael Chapman, "Children's Prosocial Dispositions and Behaviors," in *Handbook of Child Psychology*, vol. 4, *Socialization, Personality, and Social Development,* ed. E. Mavis Hetherington (New York: Wiley, 1983), 469–545.

80. Sroufe and Fleeson, "Attachment and the Construction of Relationships."

81. Craig H. Hart, Gary W. Ladd, and Brant R. Burleson, "Children's Expectations of the Outcomes of Social Strategies: Relations with Sociometric Status and Maternal Disciplinary Styles," *Child Development* 61, no. 1 (1990): 127–37.

82. Louise Bates Ames, *Raising Good Kids* (New York: Delta, 1992), 27.

83. Gary W. Ladd, Joseph M. Price, and Craig H. Hart, "Predicting Preschoolers' Peer Status from Their Playground Behaviors," *Child Development* 59, no. 4 (1988): 986–92.

84. Gary W. Ladd, "Having Friends, Keeping Friends, Making Friends, and Being Liked by Peers in the Classroom: Predictors of Children's Early School Adjustment," *Child Development* 61, no. 4 (1990): 1081–1100.

85. Willard W. Hartup, "Presidential Address. The Company They Keep: Friendships and Their Developmental Significance," *Child Development* 67 (1996): 1–13.

86. Allison Fairchild, "A New View on Child Development," *Minnesota Parent* 8, no. 83 (December 1993): 4.

87. Jacqueline J. Goodnow and W. Andrew Collins, *Development According to Parents: The Nature, Sources, and Consequences of Parents' Ideas* (Hillsdale, N.J.: Lawrence Erlbaum, 1990).

Chapter 6

88. Cynthia Cole and Hyman Rodman, "When School-Age Children Care for Themselves: Issues for Family Life Educators and Parents," *Family Relations* 26 (1987): 92–96.

89. Laurence Steinberg, "Latchkey Children and Susceptibility to Peer Pressure: An Ecological Analysis," *Developmental Psychology* 22 (1986): 433–39.

90. Earl C. Butterfield and Gary N. Siperstein, "Influence of Contingent Auditory Stimulation on Non-Nutritional Suckle," in *Third Symposium on Oral Sensation and Perception: The Mouth of the Infant,* ed. James F. Bosma (Springfield, Ill.: Charles C. Thomas, 1972).

91. Helmut Moog, *The Musical Experience of the Pre-School Child* (London: Schott, 1976).

92. Robert H. Bradley, Bettye M. Caldwell, and Stephen L. Rock, "Home Environment and School Performance: A Ten-Year Follow-up Examination of Three Models of Environmental Action," *Child Development* 59 (1988): 852–67.

93. Rebecca N. Saito, Peter L. Benson, Dale A. Blyth, and Anu R. Sharma, *Places to Grow: Perspectives on Youth Development Opportunities for 7–14 Year Old Minneapolis Youth* (Minneapolis: Search Institute, 1995), 10.

94. Ibid.

95. See, e.g., Bradley R. Hertel and Michael Hughes, "Religious Affiliation, Attendance, and Support for 'Pro-Family' Issues in the United States," *Social Forces* 65 (1987): 858–82.

96. Thomas Armstrong, *Awakening Your Child's Natural Genius* (New York: Jeremy P. Tarcher/Perigree, 1991), 151.

97. For more information about the impact of involvement in religious institutions, see Benson, *Creating Healthy Communities for Children and Adolescents*; see also Eugene C. Roehlkepartain, *Building Assets in Congregations*, pilot ed. (Minneapolis: Search Institute, 1996).

98. Michael J. Donahue and Peter L. Benson, "Religion and the Well-Being of Adolescents," *Journal of Social Issues* 51 (1995): 145–60.

99. Stanley I. Greenspan, *Playground Politics: Understanding the Emotional Life of Your School-Age Child* (Reading, Mass.: Addison-Wesley, 1993), 26.

100. Lilian G. Katz, "Overloaded Kids," *Parents* 66, no. 3 (March 1991): 186.

101. American Academy of Pediatrics, *Caring for Your School-Age Child* (New York: Bantam, 1995), 306.

102. Wendy Wood, Frank Y. Wong, and J. Gregory Chachere, "Effects of Media Violence on Viewers' Aggression in Unconstrained Social Interaction," *Psychological Bulletin* 109, no. 3 (1991): 371–83.

103. NAEYC Position Statement: Media Violence in Children's Lives, adopted April 1990, in *NAEYC Position Statements: Current as of January 1996* (Washington, D.C.: National Association for the Education of Young Children, 1990), 76.

104. Leonard D. Eron, L. Rowell Huesmann, Monroe M. Lefkowitz, and Leopold O. Walder, "Does Television Violence Cause Aggression?" *American Psychologist* 27 (1972): 253–63.

105. W. Andrew Collins, Brian L. Sobol, and Sally Westby, "Effects of Adult Commentary on Children's Comprehension and Inferences about a Televised Aggressive Portrayal," *Child Development* 52 (1981): 158–63; Leonard D. Eron and L. Rowell Huesmann, "The Control of Aggressive Behavior by Changes in Attitudes, Values, and the Conditions of Learning," in *Advances in the Study of Aggression*, vol. 2, ed. Robert J. Blanchard and Caroline Blanchard (Orlando, Fla.: Academic, 1984).

Chapter 7

106. Alfie Kohn, *Punished by Rewards: The Trouble with Gold Stars, Incentive Plans, A's, and Other Bribes* (Boston: Houghton Mifflin, 1993).

107. Carnegie Task Force on Learning in the Primary Grades, *Years of Promise: A Comprehensive Learning Strategy for America's Children* (New York: Carnegie Corporation of New York, 1996), 29.

108. Carnegie Task Force on Learning in the Primary Grades, *Years of Promise*, 132–35.

109. Reginald M. Clark, *Family Life and School Achievement: Why Poor Black Children Succeed or Fail* (Chicago: University of Chicago Press, 1983), 197–208.

110. Matas, Arend, and Sroufe, "Continuity of Adaptation."

111. David C. McClelland, John W. Atkinson, Reginald A. Clark, and Edgar L. Lowell, *The Achievement Motive* (East Norwalk, Conn.: Appleton-Century-Crofts, 1953).

112. Susan Harter, "A New Self-Report Scale of Intrinsic Versus Extrinsic Orientation in the Classroom: Motivational and Informational Components," *Developmental Psychology* 17 (1981): 300–12.

113. Martin S. Banks and Phillip Salapatek, "Infant Visual Perception," in *Handbook of Child Psychology*, vol. 2, *Infancy and Developmental Psychobiology,* ed. Marshall M. Haith and Joseph J. Campos (New York: Wiley, 1983), 435–571.

114. Leon J. Yarrow, Robert H. MacTurk, Peter M. Vietze, Mary E. McCarthy, R. P. Klein, and Susan McQuiston, "Developmental Course of Parental Stimulation and Its Relationship to Mastery Motivation During Infancy," *Developmental Psychology* 20 (1984): 492–503.

115. Judy Dunn, *Distress and Comfort* (Cambridge, Mass.: Harvard University Press, 1977).

116. Bettye M. Caldwell and Robert H. Bradley, *Manual for the Home Observation for Measurement of the Environment* (Little Rock: University of Arkansas Press, 1984); Allen W. Gottfried, "Home Environment and Early Cognitive Development: Integration, Meta-Analyses, and Conclusions," in *Home Environment and Early Cognitive Development: Longitudinal Research,* ed. Allen W. Gottfried (Orlando, Fla.: Academic, 1984).

117. Victor Groze and Daruela Ileana, "*A Follow-up Study of Adopted Children from Romania,*" paper presented at the 21st Annual North American Council on Adoptable Children Conference, Norfolk, Va., August 1995.

118. Michael Rutter, "Special Report: International Conference on Infant Studies, Romanian Orphans Adopted Early Overcome Deprivation," *Brown University Child and Adolescent Behavior Letter* 12, no. 6 (June 1996).

119. Bradley, Caldwell, and Rock, "Home Environment and School Performance," 852–67.

120. Keith O. Yeates, David MacPhee, Frances A. Campbell, and Craig T. Ramey, "Maternal IQ and Home Environments as Determinants of Early Childhood Intellectual Competence: A Developmental Analysis," *Developmental Psychology* 19 (1983): 731–39.

121. Daisy Edmondson, "Bulletin: Letting Children Do It Their Way," *Parents* 69, no. 2 (February 1994): 138.

122. Diane Heacox, *Up from Underachievement* (Minneapolis: Free Spirit, 1991), 22.

123. Lynn Corno, "Homework is a Compliance Thing," *Educational Researcher* 25, no. 8 (1996): 27–30.

124. J. David Hawkins and Joseph G. Weis, "The Social Development Model: An Integrated Approach to Delinquency Prevention," *Journal of Primary Prevention* 7 (1985): 73–97; Kathy McNamara, "Bonding to School and the Development of Responsibility," *Journal of Emotional and Behavioral Problems* 4, no. 4 (1996): 33–35; Carole Ames, "Classroom: Goals, Structures, and Student Motivation," *Journal of Educational Psychology* 84 (1992): 261–71; S. A. Cernkovich and P. C. Giordano, "School Bonding, Race, and Delinquency," *Criminology* 30, no. 2 (1992): 261–91.

125. Barbara D. DeBaryshe, "Joint Picture-Book Reading Correlates of Early Oral Language Skill," *Journal of Child Language* 20, no. 2 (1993): 455–61.

126. Mary R. Jalongo and Melissa A. Renck, "Children's Literature and the Child's Adjustment to School," *Reading Teacher* 40, no. 7 (1987): 616–21.

127. Joanne Oppenheim, Barbara Brenner, and Betty D. Boegehold, *Choosing Books for Kids: Choosing the Right Book for the Right Child at the Right Time* (New York: Ballantine, 1986).

128. Ibid.

129. Richard W. Riley, *Make a Difference in 30 Minutes a Day* (Washington, D.C.: U.S. Department of Education, 1995).

130. Jim Trelease, *The Read-Aloud Handbook* (New York: Penguin, 1995), 45.

Chapter 8

131. Harriet L. Rheingold, "Little Children's Participation in the Work of Adults, and Nascent Prosocial Behavior," *Child Development* 53 (1982): 114–25.

132. Carolyn Zahn-Waxler, Marian Radke-Yarrow, Elizabeth Wagner, and Michael Chapman, "Development of Concern for Others," *Developmental Psychology* 28 (1992): 163–72.

133. Marian Radke-Yarrow and Carolyn Zahn-Waxler, "The Role of Familial Factors in the Development of Prosocial Behavior: Research Findings and Questions," in *Development of Antisocial and Prosocial Behavior,* ed. Dan Olweus, Jack Block, and Marian Radke-Yarrow (Orlando, Fla.: Academic, 1986).

134. David A. Hamburg, *Today's Children: Creating a Future for a Generation in Crisis* (New York: Random House, 1992).

135. Bill Underwood and Bert Moore, "Perspective-Taking and Altruism," *Psychological Bulletin* 91 (1982): 143–73.

136. Benson, *Developmental Assets among Minneapolis Youth;* Benson, *Developmental Assets among Albuquerque Youth.*

137. Stephen L. Carter, *Integrity* (New York: Basic, 1996), 7.

138. Harlan S. Hansen, *Teaching Responsibility to Young Children* (River Forest, Ill.: LEA/DECE, 1982), 9.

139. Ibid., 11.

140. Laurence Steinberg, "Familial Factors in Delinquency: A Developmental Perspective," *Journal of Adolescent Research* 2, no. 3 (1987): 255–68.

141. Eleanor E. Maccoby, "Middle Childhood in the Context of the Family," in *Development During Middle Childhood: The Years Six to Twelve,* ed. W. Andrew Collins (Washington, D.C.: National Academy of Sciences Press, 1984), 184–239.

142. See, e.g., Anne C. Petersen and Nancy Leffert, "Developmental Issues Influencing Guidelines for Adolescent Health Research: A Review," *Journal of Adolescent Health* 17 (1995): 298–305.

143. Anne C. Bernstein, *Flight of the Stork* (Indianapolis: Perspectives Press, 1994), 124.

144. See, e.g., Peter C. Scales, "The Centrality of Health Education to Adolescents' Critical Thinking," *Journal of Health Education* 24, no. 6 (1993): 510–14.

145. Robert Coles, "Raising a Moral Child," *Sesame Street Parents* 236 (July/August 1994): 14.

146. American Academy of Pediatrics, *Caring for Your Baby and Young Child: Birth to Age 5* (New York: Bantam, 1993), 268.

Chapter 9

147. Kevin J. Swick and Tammy Hassell, "Parental Efficacy and the Development of Social Competence in Young Children," *Journal of Instructional Psychology* 17, no. 1 (1990): 24–32.

148. Lisa S. Freund, "Maternal Regulation of Children's Problem-Solving Behavior and Its Impact on Children's Performance," *Child Development* 61 (1990): 113–26.

149. Teresa M. Amabile, *Growing Up Creative* (New York: Crown, 1989), 4.

150. Ibid., 63.

151. Joal Hetherington, "The Scoop on Groups," *Child* 6, no. 6 (August 1991): 48.

152. Robert L. Selman, "Social-Cognitive Understanding: A Guide to Educational and Clinical Practice," in *Moral Development and Behavior: Theory, Research, and Social Issues,* ed. Thomas Likona (New York: Holt, Rinehart, and Winston, 1976).

153. In Rhoda Metraux, ed., *Margaret Mead: Some Personal Views* (New York: Walker, 1979), 202.

154. Daniel Goleman, *Emotional Intelligence.*

155. Judy Dunn, Jane Brown, and Lynn Beardsall, "Family Talk about Feeling States and Children's Later Understanding of Children's Emotions," *Developmental Psychology* 27 (1991): 448–55.

156. See Benson, *Creating Healthy Communities for Children and Adolescents.*

157. Frances E. Aboud, *Children and Prejudice* (New York: Basil Blackwell, 1988).

158. Frances E. Aboud, "A Test of Ethnocentrism with Young Children," *Canadian Journal of Behavioural Science* 12 (1980), 195–209.

159. Darlene Powell Hopson and Derek S. Hopson, *Different and Wonderful: Raising Black Children in a Race-Conscious Society* (New York: Fireside, 1990), 43.

160. Aboud, *Children and Prejudice.*

161. Ibid., 20.

162. See, e.g., Gilbert J. Botvin, Eli Baker, Anne D. Filazzola, and Elizabeth Botvin, "A Cognitive-Behavioral Approach to Substance Use Prevention: One Year Follow-up," *Addictive Behaviors* 15 (1990): 47–63.

163. Charles L. Whitfield, *Boundaries and Relationships* (Deerfield Beach, Fla.: Health Communications, 1993).

164. Ibid., 68–69.

165. Charles Brenner, *An Elementary Textbook of Psychoanalysis* (Garden City, N.Y.: Doubleday, 1974).

166. Whitfield, *Boundaries and Relationships.*

167. J. Ronald Lally, "What to Do About Hitting," *Parents* 69, no. 7 (July 1994): 64.

168. Willard W. Hartup, "Aggression in Childhood: Developmental Perspectives," *American Psychologist* 29 (1974), 336–41.

169. Gerald R. Patterson, "Mothers: The Unacknowledged Victims," *Monographs of the Society for Research on Child Development* 45, no. 5, serial No. 186 (1991); Gerald R. Patterson, *Coercive Family Processes* (Eugene, Ore.: Castilia, 1982).

170. Gerald R. Patterson, Barbara D. DeBaryshe, and Elizabeth Ramsey, "A Developmental Perspective on Antisocial Behavior," *American Psychologist* 44 (1989): 329–35.

Chapter 10

171. Erik H. Erikson, *Childhood and Society,* 2d ed. (New York: Norton, 1963).

172. Martin E. P. Seligman, *The Optimistic Child* (Boston: Houghton Mifflin, 1995), 10.

173. Collins, Harris, and Susman, "Parenting During Middle Childhood," 66.

174. Grayson N. Holmbeck, Roberta L. Paikoff, and Jeanne Brooks-Gunn, "Parenting Adolescents," in *Handbook of Parenting,* vol. 1, *Children and Parenting*, ed. Marc H. Bornstein (Mahwah, N.J.: Lawrence Erlbaum, 1995), 91–118.

175. Maccoby, "Middle Childhood in the Context of the Family."

176. Susan Nolen-Hoeksema and Jean S. Girgus, "The Emergence of Gender Differences in Depression During Adolescence," *Psychological Bulletin* 115 (1994): 424–43.

177. Bruce E. Compas, "Coping with Stress During Childhood and Adolescence," *Psychological Bulletin* 101 (1987): 393–403.

178. Julian B. Rotter, "Some Problems and Misconceptions Related to the Construct of Internal vs. External Control of Reinforcement," *Journal of Consulting and Clinical Trials* 43 (1975): 56–67. John S. Cartou, Stephen Nowicki, and Ginger M. Balses, "An Observational Study of Antecedents of Locus of Control of Reinforcement," *International Journal of Behavioral Development* 19, no. 1 (1996): 161–75.

179. Susan Harter and James P. Connell, "A Comparision of Alternative Models of the Relationships Between Academic Achievement and Children's Perceptions of Competence, Control, and Motivational Orientation," in *The Development of Achievement-Related Cognitions and Behavior,* ed. J. Nichols (Greenwich, Conn.: JAI, 1982).

180. Kenneth H. Rubin and Linda Rose Krasnor, "Social-Cognitive and Social Behavioral Perspectives on Problem Solving," in *Minnesota Symposia on Child Psychology,* vol. 18, ed. Marion Pearlmutter (Hillsdale, N.J.: Lawrence Erlbaum, 1986): 1–68.

181. Sigrun Adalbjarnardottir, "How Schoolchildren Propose to Negotiate: The Role of Social Withdrawal, Social Anxiety, and Locus of Control," *Child Development* 66, no. 6 (1995): 1739–51.

182. Susan Harter, "Self and Identity Development," in At the Threshold: The Developing Adolescent," ed. Shirley S. Feldman and Glen R. Elliott (Cambridge, Mass.: Harvard University Press, 1990), 353–87.

183. Richard M. Lerner, America's Youth in Crisis: Challenges and Options for Programs and Policies (Thousand Oaks, Calif.: Sage, 1995).

184. Nancy E. Curry and Carl N. Johnson, *Beyond Self-Esteem: Developing a Genuine Sense of Human Value* (Washington, D.C.: National Association for the Education of Young Children, 1990), 8–9.

185. Harter, "Self and Identity Development."

186. Ibid.

187. Roberta S. Isberg, Stuart T. Hauser, Alan M. Jacobson, et al., "Parental Contexts of Adolescent Self-Esteem: A Developmental Perspective," *Journal of Youth and Adolescence* 18 (1989): 1–23.

188. Karin S. Frey and Diane N. Ruble, "What Children Say When the Teacher Is Not Around: Conflicting Goals in Social Comparison and Performance Assessment in the Classroom," *Journal of Personality and Social Psychology* 48 (1985): 550–62.

189. Louise Hart, *The Winning Family: Increasing Self-Esteem in Your Children and Yourself* (Berkeley, Calif.: Celestial Arts, 1987), 10.

190. Roberta G. Simmons and Dale A. Blyth, *Moving into Adolescence: The Impact of Pubertal Change and School Context* (New York: Aldine de Gruyter, 1987); Anne C. Petersen, "Adolescent Development," *Annual Review of Psychology* 39 (1988): 583–607; Hakan Stattin and David Magnusson, *Pubertal Maturation in Female Develoment,* vol. 2, *Paths Through Life* (Hillsdale, N.J.: Lawrence Erlbaum, 1990).

191. Carol Gilligan, Nona P. Lyons, and Trudy J. Hanmer, eds., *Making Connections: The Relational Worlds of Adolescent Girls at Emma Willard School* (Cambridge, Mass.: Harvard University Press, 1990), 10.

192. Ibid.

193. Simmons and Blyth, *Moving into Adolescence;* Petersen, "Adolescent Development"; Stattin and Magnusson, *Pubertal Maturation in Female Development.*

194. Seligman, *The Optimistic Child,* 297.

195. Ibid.

196. Ibid.

197. Ibid.

Chapter 11

198. Marian Wright Edelman, *The Measure of Our Success* (Boston: Beacon, 1992), 53.

Recommended Reading

Caring for Your Baby and Young Child: Birth to Age 5, by the American Academy of Pediatrics, Bantam, 1993.

Caring for Your School-Age Child: Ages 5 to 12, by the American Academy of Pediatrics, Bantam, 1995.

Daycare (revised ed.), by A. Clarke-Stewart, Harvard University Press, 1993.

Emotional Intelligence, by Daniel Goleman, Bantam, 1995.

Flight of the Stork, by Anne C. Bernstein, Perspectives Press, 1994.

First Feelings: Milestones in the Emotional Development of Your Baby and Child, by Stanley I. Greenspan and Nancy Thorndike Greenspan, Viking, 1985.

The First Twelve Months of Life: Your Baby's Growth Month by Month, by the Princeton Center for Infancy and Early Childhood, Grosset, 1973.

Growing Up Creative, by Teresa M. Amabile, Ph.D., Creative Education Foundation Press, 1989.

The Hurried Child, by David Elkind, Addison-Wesley, 1981.

Infants and Mothers: Differences in Development, by T. Berry Brazelton, Delacorte, 1983.

The New First Three Years of Life, by Burton L. White, Fireside, 1995.

The Optimistic Child, by Martin E. P. Seligman, Houghton Mifflin, 1995.

Starting Points: Meeting the Needs of Our Youngest Children, by the Carnegie Task Force on Meeting the Needs of Young Children, Carnegie Corporation of New York, 1994.

The State of America's Children Yearbook, written and published by the Children's Defense Fund, 1995.

Teaching Your Child Values, by Linda and Richard Eyre, Fireside, 1993.

Toddlers and Parents: A Declaration of Independence, by T. Berry Brazelton, Delta, 1989.

Touchpoints: Your Child's Emotional and Behavioral Development, by T. Berry Brazelton, Addison-Wesley, 1992.

What to Expect the First Year, by Arlene Eisenberg, Heidi E. Murkoff, and Sandee E. Hathaway, Workman Publishing, 1989.

What to Expect: the Toddler Years, by Arlene Eisenberg, Heidi E. Murkoff, and Sandee E. Hathaway, Workman Publishing, 1994.

Years of Promise: A Comprehensive Learning Strategy for America's Children, by the Carnegie Task Force on Learning in the Primary Grades, Carnegie Corporation of New York, 1996.

Your Baby and Child from Birth to Age 5, by Penelope Leach, Knopf, 1989.

Asset-Building Resources from Search Institute

Search Institute is developing a wide range of resources to assist individuals, organizations, and communities in asset-building efforts. While most of these resources focus on adolescents, many of the principles and ideas can be translated into asset-building efforts for children. For more information or a catalog of additional resources, call 1-800-888-7828 or visit Search Institute's web site at: www.search-institute.org

▼ Resources For Understanding Assets

The Troubled Journey: A Portrait of 6th–12th Grade Youth
by Dr. Peter L. Benson

This in-depth, groundbreaking report provides the original research framework for an asset-promoting approach. Using surveys of almost 47,000 6th- to 12th-graders, this report proposes a vision for positive youth development, defines developmental assets, and shows how assets guide youth in making wise choices and avoiding risky behavior.

Creating Healthy Communities for Children and Adolescents *(tentative title)*
by Dr. Peter L. Benson

This new book provides a comprehensive presentation of the developmental assets; it is forthcoming from Jossey-Bass in late 1997.

Healthy Communities, Healthy Youth
by Dr. Dale A. Blyth with Eugene C. Roehlkepartain

This report examines important community strengths and highlights the impact of community health on vulnerable youth. It also proposes strategies for parents, educators, and others who are working to strengthen their communities.

Profiles of Student Life: Attitudes and Behaviors

Hundreds of schools and dozens of community-wide initiatives across the United States use data from this survey to develop asset-building strategies and to create positive new visions for their youth. This survey is unique because it focuses on grades 6 through 12 and looks at the assets young people need to grow up healthy.

▼ Ideas for Building Assets

Uniting Communities for Youth: Mobilizing All Sectors to Create a Positive Future
by Dr. Peter L. Benson

This introductory booklet calls communities to rally around young people with a positive vision for asset building. The booklet demonstrates the power of developmental assets and recommends strategies for getting started.

Finding a Focus: Rethinking the Public Sector's Role in Building Assets in Youth
by Hope Melton and Eugene C. Roehlkepartain

This booklet explores the possibilities and suggests specific strategies for ways leaders in the public sector can become catalysis for uniting communities for youth.

Learning and Living: How Asset Building for Youth Can Unify a School's Mission
by Dr. Donald Draayer and Eugene C. Roehlkepartain

This booklet helps superintendents, principals, teachers, counselors, and other school staff understand their role as asset builders from a perspective of total student development.

Parenting with a Purpose: A Positive Approach for Raising Confident, Caring Youth
by Dean Feldmeyer and Eugene C. Roehlkepartain

This booklet challenges parents to view parenting through the asset framework, highlighting how the assets can reshape major parenting tasks and suggesting ways parents can find support in the community.

Renewing Hope: Strengthening Community-Based Organizations' Role in Helping Youth Thrive
by Laura Lee M. Geraghty and Eugene C. Roehlkepartain

This booklet provides a framework for rethinking priorities and suggests strategies for building assets through the organization's programs, in employees' families, and in community-wide efforts.

Tapping the Potential: Discovering Congregations' Role in Building Assets in Youth
by Glenn A. Seefeldt and Eugene C. Roehlkepartain

This booklet encourages congregations to rethink their youth programs and calls congregations to become advocates and catalysts on behalf of all youth in their communities.

240 Ideas for Building Assets in Youth

This informational, eye-catching poster offers practical and easy ideas that anyone can use to help build developmental assets.

Building Assets in Youth Video
featuring Dr. Peter L. Benson

This 12-minute video presents the vision of asset-building communities, describes the impact of asset building, and motivates people to get started.

Building Assets Together
by Jolene L. Roehlkepartain

This book gives creative, easy-to-use activities to introduce developmental assets to youth. It includes 70 interactive group activities and 31 attractive, photocopiable worksheets that help youth understand their own assets.

150 Ways to Show Kids You Care
by Jolene L. Roehlkepartain

This unique handout inspires and motivates adults with practical ideas for showing kids they care.

What Kids Need to Succeed
by Dr. Peter L. Benson, Judy Galbraith, and Pamela Espeland

This easy-to-read book presents the developmental assets, shows their importance to helping youth make positive life choices, and gives practical ideas for building each one.

Ideas for Parents Newsletters Master Set
by Jolene L. Roehlkepartain

This set of 37 newsletter masters lets communities or organizations provide parents with practical tips to help their children grow into responsible, successful adults.

Comment Form: Comments about Developmental Assets for Children

Starting Out Right is our first attempt to create developmental assets for children. We invite dialogue on this subject. Please photocopy this form and share with us your reactions to the material presented in this report. We will consider your ideas as Search Institute continues to develop assets for children.

Name _____

Address _____

City _____ State _____ Zip _____

Daytime phone _____ E-mail address: _____

What is your general reaction to *Starting Out Right*? _____

_____

What is most useful about the framework of children's assets? _____

_____

What would make this report even more useful for you? _____

_____

How would you strengthen the asset framework for children? _____

_____

What additional research and practical resources would you like to see on children's developmental assets?

_____

Send a photocopy of this form to:
Nancy Leffert, Ph.D.
Search Institute
700 South Third Street, Suite 210
Minneapolis, MN 55415-1138
fax: (612) 376-8956
email: nleffert@search-institute.org

▼ About the Authors

Nancy Leffert, Ph.D., is a research scientist at Search Institute. She earned her doctorate in child psychology from the Institute of Child Development, University of Minnesota, and a master's degree in social work from San Diego State University. She is particularly interested in the effects of community contexts on the transition to adolescence and the role of pubertal development among special populations, particularly young people with Attention Deficit Hyperactivity Disorder, learning disabilities, and affective disorders. She also is a licensed independent social worker, and the author of many articles and book chapters on development.

Peter L. Benson, Ph.D., who first conceptualized the framework of developmental assets for adolescents, has been president of Search Institute since 1985. He is the author and coauthor of numerous books and reports on adolescents, including *Uniting Communities for Youth* (Search Institute, 1995), *The Troubled Journey: A Portrait of 6th–12th Grade Youth* (Search Institute, 1990, 1993), *What Kids Need to Succeed,* with Judy Galbraith and Pamela Espeland (Free Spirit, 1995), and *The Quicksilver Years: The Hopes and Fears of Early Adolescence* (Harper & Row, 1987).

Jolene L. Roehlkepartain is a writer and editor who specializes in parenting and education issues. She is the author of a dozen books and curricula for parents, educators, youth, and youth workers, including *Building Assets Together* (Search Institute, 1995), *Fidget Busters* (Group Publishing, 1992), and *Surviving School Stress* (Teenage Books, 1990). She has worked with children and youth for 17 years and is the founding editor of *Adoptive Families* magazine and the former editor of *Parents of Teenagers* and *Teenage* magazine.

▼ About Search Institute

Search Institute is a nonprofit, nonsectarian research and educational organization that advances the well-being and positive development of children and youth through applied research, evaluation, consultation, training, and the development of publications and practical resources for educators, youth-serving professionals, parents, community leaders, and policy makers. For a free information packet, call 1-800-888-7828. Or see Search Institute's web site (http://www.search-institute.org).